S0-EAO-661

Welcome to *WorkWise: Getting a Job.*

Landing a new job can be very difficult, but it is not impossible. If you plan and prepare in smart ways, you can find the right job. If you completed *WorkWise: Choosing a Job*, you have already boosted your confidence, defined your ideal job, and written your résumé. Now it's time to show employers that you can be a great employee.

In this workbook, you will learn about three steps that will help you to get a good job:

- Conducting the Job Search: Knowing where and how to look will help you to find the best opportunities.

- Preparing for Interviews: Learning how to prepare and practice for your interviews will make you a standout candidate.

- Interviewing to Win: Presenting yourself well in interviews will help employers to see you as the right candidate.

Just by starting this workbook, you are making progress toward your new career. This is your workbook. To learn the most from this workbook, you will need to work! Each lesson has exercises to help you think deeply. Take your time and do all the exercises.

You will have space to write down your thoughts, and you can go back to review them at any time. You may want to use a pencil, so you can change your answers as you learn more. You may also want to reread some lessons or do some exercises over again. Take your time. These exercises will help you set a strong path to finding a career and getting a new job.

On some pages, you will see definitions of words that may be new to you. If you find other words that you are unsure of, look up the definitions and write them down. There is room in the margin for you to add more definitions or to make notes of sections you want to revisit.

Many exercises and worksheets are included within this book. You can find more worksheets and tools at the New Readers Press website. Go to www.newreaderspress.com/workwise to print out these tools and to find links to the online resources mentioned in this book.

Self-Check: My Goals

Read each statement. Check the ones that apply to you. Then complete the sentence about what you hope to learn from this workbook.

- ☐ I have never had a paid job.
- ☐ I have never applied for a job.
- ☐ I am not sure where to find jobs.
- ☐ I have never had a formal job interview.
- ☐ I am scared to go to job interviews.
- ☐ I have applied for many jobs, but I have not been hired.
- ☐ I'm not sure I want a new job, but I have to read this book for class.

I hope to learn _____

_____

Where do you find jobs? This is a harder question than it seems. Many people just check job ads. However, there are many other—and better—places to find jobs.

You should look at job ads, but keep in mind that most jobs are not found that way. To increase your chances of getting a job, try to find job openings before they are advertised. In this unit, you will learn about the following:

- Understanding the Hiring Process – Lesson 1

- Looking in the Best Places – Lesson 2

- **Networking** Your Way to a Job – Lesson 3

networking – talking with people in similar jobs to share ideas

Job seekers often struggle to find the right opportunities and to get job interviews. In this unit, you will learn ways to overcome both of these struggles. Your goal is to get more job opportunities and more interviews.

Exercise: How I Found Jobs

Write a sentence about how you found a job, or ask someone you know how she or he found a job. Did you answer a job ad? Did someone you know tell you about the job?

_____

_____

_____

Some job seekers spend many hours checking online employment websites and submitting résumés, but they get few or no responses. You will have more success if you spend time networking, which you will learn about in this unit.

Self-Check: How Do People Find Jobs?

Read the ways people find jobs. What do they do? Check the ideas that you think work.

- ☐ Answer an ad in the newspaper or online.
- ☐ Hear about a job from a friend.
- ☐ Go to job fairs.
- ☐ Look for opportunities to volunteer.
- ☐ Know how employers hire people.
- ☐ Talk to friends of friends.
- ☐ Ask for help.

How many statements did you check? _____

After you read lessons 1, 2, and 3, take the self-check again. See if your answers change.

Lesson 1   Understanding the Hiring Process

What is the hiring process? To begin your job search, first understand how employees are hired. Have you ever thought about how a job gets created? Employers don't hire people because they like them. Employers hire people to solve a problem, to fill a need, and to make money for the company.

Therefore, employers go through a long, thoughtful process to decide to create a job and hire someone for it. Larger companies usually have a longer process, while small businesses may have a shorter process. Here are some common steps an employer takes.

Step 1: Identify a business need.

During this step, the employer identifies a need that the business has to keep doing well or to grow. Some business needs include:

- Increasing sales
- Improving customer satisfaction
- Increasing productivity or quality
- Reducing costs
- Reducing defects or problems
- Following government regulations
- Training employees
- Explaining their products or services to customers or clients

productivity – the rate at which work is completed

defects – flaws or problems with a product

regulations – rules that must be followed

products – items that a business makes or sells

services – work that you pay a business to do

Exercise: What Problems or Services Can I Solve for an Employer?

Think about your skills and knowledge. Now think about a business you know. What problems or needs could you solve if you worked for the business?

_____

_____

_____

_____

Step 2: Explore potential solutions, calculate the cost of each solution, and decide which solution is most cost-effective.

cost-effective – costing the least amount of money over time

An employer must think carefully about how to address a business need or problem. Often, many people at a company will look at a variety of solutions and determine how much each solution will cost over time. That is a good way to compare the ideas and choose the right one. For example, a restaurant may have a problem during lunch service. The restaurant needs to serve more customers quickly at lunchtime.

- One option is not to change anything.

  This option may seem to be the least expensive, but the restaurant may actually lose money. What if many potential customers go to other places because the restaurant is too busy at lunchtime? If just 20 people who spend $15 each go somewhere else, the restaurant could lose $300 per day.

- Another option is to put in a "Grab and Go" section with ready-made foods that can be purchased at the counter.

  This could be a good idea, but the restaurant must make sure it is supplying the food that customers want. If it doesn't choose the right meals, the Grab and Go lunches could spoil. The restaurant could lose more money. The current staff will also need to work the Grab and Go counter, while still waiting on customers sitting in the restaurant.

- A third option is to hire another server to work during lunch.

  This option could be a good solution if the restaurant hires an experienced server who can take care of many customers during a busy shift. If so, the restaurant can make more than what it costs to hire the new server. If the new person serves 20 more customers, the restaurant may make $300 extra per day. If the server is paid $60 for each lunch shift, that would make the new position worth the cost.

Step 3: Decide to create a position, and define the job requirements.

bottom line – how much money a company makes after subtracting expenses

Once a business determines that hiring a new employee is best for the bottom line, the position will need to be defined. The employer needs to figure out the job requirements and describe what the new employee will do. The hiring manager will think about the job carefully and decide what qualifications are the most important. These are some possible job qualifications:

- Work experience
- Personality
- Credentials
- Accomplishments
- Education

Managers will rank the qualifications by what is most important. Then they will use the qualifications to write a job description.

Step 4: Set a budget and work with the human resources department.

benefits – extra things that companies provide to their workers in addition to pay

Now the employer must figure out how much money it can spend on the new employee. This will include pay, benefits, and training. If the employer is a large company, it will have a human resources (HR) manager, who is in charge of hiring employees and managing their benefits. With small businesses, the owner may also have to do the HR work, but he or she still will need to think about all the steps in hiring a person.

Step 5: Advertise the position.

At this step, the employer will post the position in the newspaper or on job websites.

However, many employers do not reach this step because they will first consider people from a pool of "best-known candidates." These are people that other employees, clients, or suppliers will recommend for the job. If one of these candidates fits the new job, the company will likely hire that person. And then the company has less work to do to find a new employee.

candidates – people who are being considered for a job

If the company does not find someone through this list, then the job is posted. But keep in mind, jobs may still be posted even when an employer has best-known candidates to interview. When you read a job ad, you do not know whether the employer already has someone in mind or not. This is why you should aim to become one of the best-known candidates.

Step 6: Review résumés and applications.

At this point, the employer may have hundreds or thousands of résumés and applications to review. Many companies will use applicant tracking software on their computers to review résumés for keywords, and only résumés with enough keywords will be read by an actual person.

keywords – words used in a job ad or by an industry to describe job requirements

Exercise: Identify Keywords in an Ad

Position Summary: Pipefitter

summary – short statement of the main points

- Lay out, position, align, and fit together fabricated parts
- Read and interpret blueprints, field sketches, and specifications
- Fabricate and install screw pipe, socket weld pipe, stainless tubing, carbon steel weld pipe, stainless steel weld pipe
- Install valves, underground pipe, pipe hangers, and supports
- Steam and heat tracing
- Basic plumbing repair
- Minor valve maintenance and repair
- Test piping systems
- Operate pneumatic and electric tools
- Leak test tubing systems
- Minimum 4 years of industrial construction/maintenance experience

On the lines below, list some keywords from the ad.

_____

_____

_____

Did you notice that the word *pipe* was used many times? If you sent a résumé without the keyword *pipe* in it, do you think you would be called for an interview?

Step 7: Interview candidates.

After reviewing résumés, an employer will often pick five or six candidates to interview. In large companies, people in HR usually conduct these interviews. Sometimes a company uses phone interviews to narrow the field of candidates before holding in-person interviews.

Step 8: Choose three top candidates.

The screening interviews help employers decide on their top candidates. Then they interview each of the candidates in person to decide which is the best fit for the job. Sometimes candidates are interviewed more than once or by more than one person in the company.

Step 9: Choose the top candidate and make a job offer.

verbal – spoken

offer letter – official letter from a company stating the pay and benefits offered for a job

Finally, after this long process, the employer chooses a candidate. The employer or HR manager may make a **verbal** offer to get feedback from the candidate. Then, if the candidate is interested in the job, the employer will send a formal **offer letter** with information about benefits and pay.

Step 10: Negotiate pay and benefits.

negotiate – talk over to agree on terms

wage – amount paid for work

salaried – being paid a fixed amount for regular work

For some jobs, the candidate and the employer may **negotiate** the pay and benefits. Many jobs, however, will have a set **wage**. And some companies offer standard benefits that cannot be negotiated. Most hourly jobs have set wages. Many **salaried** jobs involve negotiations. For some jobs, candidates may be able to negotiate a start date or hours.

Step 11: Candidate accepts offer.

If the candidate and the employer come to an agreement about the pay and benefits, the candidate will accept the job offer. If the candidate does not accept the offer, the employer may need to contact another candidate, or start the hiring process all over again.

Step 12: Complete the hiring process.

When a candidate accepts a job offer, the company may order a drug test or a background check. If both go well, the candidate is officially hired by the company. However, if the candidate fails the drug test or the background check uncovers something not tolerated by the company, the company can take back the job offer. If the company discovers that a candidate has lied on his or her résumé or application, the company may take back the offer.

Why should you care about the hiring process?

First, as you can see, the hiring process is a lot of work for an employer. When an employer meets you for an interview, he or she is hoping that you can help to fill a need or solve a problem. You want to show that you are the answer. You want the employer to believe that you can fix the problem.

Second, if you apply for a posted job, you have already missed the first few opportunities to get the job. The hiring manager may already have a candidate in mind. An employee within the company may want to move to the position. Or there may be a list of best-known candidates. You need to present yourself to stand out among these already known candidates.

Third, a company may want to hire someone as quickly as possible, especially if the opening is for an important position. This is one reason why a company looks at best-known candidates first. If you become a best-known candidate, employers may contact you before advertising a job.

Use informational interviews to find out about jobs early in the process.

In an informational interview, you meet with an HR manager or a supervisor at a company where you are interested in working. Your objective is to learn more about the type of job you want. In this interview, you do not ask for a job, instead you ask for advice on your job search.

objective – goal that takes effort to achieve

One great way to get an informational interview is by attending a meeting of people who work in your target industry. At this kind of meeting, you can network— or make connections—and get to know people. You can ask for informational interviews by saying something like this: "I would appreciate your opinion. I was wondering if we could plan a time where I could tell you about my background and get your feedback on my job search."

industry – group of companies that provide a type of service or product, such as health care, construction, retail, or hospitality

If you don't belong to an organization in your field, you might know other people who can give you information. Here are some people you could ask for informational interviews:

- Fellow members of your place of worship
- Neighbors
- Friends of friends
- Former co-workers, customers, or work contacts
- Government representatives
- Fellow members of social clubs or community organizations
- Fellow volunteers at charitable events

Think about all the people you know, and you may be surprised how many people can help you. Most people want to help. You just have to ask.

confidence – feeling or belief that you can do great things

You may not feel comfortable asking for informational interviews or selling your skills. But, with practice, your **confidence** will grow. Remember, many employers are looking for candidates like you.

When you meet with people for informational interviews, take along a notebook and pen. Listen carefully and take notes. The employer may give you new ideas or recommend that you speak with another person. An employer may even know of someone who needs your help right now. Be sure to thank people for their time and advice, even if you don't think it's helpful. Read your notes later, and follow up with the new ideas or leads you receive.

Exercise: My List of People for Informational Interviews

Think about the people you know. Think about companies where people you know work. Try to think of people who work in the type of job you want. Make a list of 5–10 people to talk with.

_____   _____

_____   _____

_____   _____

Congratulations! You have just created a starter list for networking. You'll read more about networking in Lesson 3.

Lesson 2   Looking in the Best Places

While you set up informational interviews, you should also check online and offline sources for job ads. This lesson will help you get started with your job search.

Search for jobs online.

Before the internet was widely used, most people read help wanted ads in newspapers. Now, companies post open positions online. The internet speeds up the process of finding new employees.

Here are some things to keep in mind:

1. The internet offers a world of opportunities. In fact, you may find more open positions than you can apply to.

2. Most employment websites are free for job seekers to use. If you do not have a computer with internet access at home, you may find computers to use at your local library, school, or job center.

3. Competition for online job postings is tough. Many people will see the ads and respond. An employer can get hundreds of applications for each opening.

4. Sometimes even the most qualified workers don't get an interview!

You can also check www.everyoneon.org to find low-cost internet options.

Many people don't get interviews because their résumés do not stand out. Here are some tips to improve your chances of getting an interview:

*   Be a first responder. If you are one of the first 20 people to respond to a position, you have a 1 in 20 chance of getting your résumé noticed. However, if you wait a couple of days, and hundreds of people apply, your odds go way down. Respond to openings as soon as possible. Consider subscribing to free online services, like www.indeed.com, to get emails right away when interesting jobs are posted. Check company websites often to see if they have openings.

*   Customize your résumé and cover letter. To customize your résumé and cover letter to a specific job opening, study the job description. Look for keywords that describe the qualifications or duties for the job. Use some of those keywords in your résumé and cover letter. The more keywords you can use, the greater your chances that the employer will notice your application.

customize – change something to fit someone's specific needs

qualifications – things that make a person fit for a job

*   Make an extra effort. Most companies will give directions for submitting your application and résumé for a job. However, your goal is to get the attention of the main decision-maker for the job. If you are very interested in a job opening, do some research. Find out the name of the hiring manager. Check the company website, or call the company and ask for the name of the person in charge of the department. You can also search on www.linkedin.com. Get their contact information. In addition to following the directions in the ad, also send the hiring manager your cover letter and résumé. Invite that person to join your LinkedIn network. By sending your application to two people at the company, you increase your chances of success. Taking that extra step shows the employer that you really care about the job.

You can learn more about using LinkedIn in *WorkWise: Choosing a Job.*

Use the top online sources to find jobs.

While searching online is helpful, a recent survey shows that only about 15% of all jobs are found using online job boards. If only 15% of all jobs are found online, then you shouldn't spend more than 15% of your time searching online.

1. **Employment websites.** An online employment website is an online meeting place for job seekers and hiring companies. There are many employment websites, but these two sites include listings from all the other sites:

- www.indeed.com
- www.simplyhired.com

> You can find job search tools at these websites.

Online employment sites allow job seekers to search thousands of job openings for free. You can search jobs by job title, keyword, and location.

For example, if you want to work as a hotel front desk clerk in Kansas City, Missouri, you can type in *Hotel Front Desk Clerk* for keywords and *Kansas City, MO* for location. Often, you can also use your zip code in the location search. After you enter your search, the site will show you a list of advertised jobs.

Some employment websites will allow you to set up email alerts when certain types of jobs are posted. You can get emails every week or even every day from these sites. Local newspapers will also have employment sections on their websites.

> You can find a local job center using this website.

In addition to online job sites, there are local job centers that help unemployed workers. Look for one near you by checking this website: www.careeronestop.org. Click on "find local help" to find centers and services near you. When you go to the job center, ask for help posting your résumé online, and someone can show you how to apply online for jobs.

2. **Company websites.** If you read *WorkWise: Choosing a Job*, you have created a list of **prospective** employers where you would like to work. If you have not, take some time now to list about 10 employers in your area where you might like to work. See the exercise on page 13.

> **prospective** – potential, likely to happen

Sometimes employers do not advertise jobs on employment websites because it costs them money. Instead they may just post jobs on their own website. Make a habit of visiting the sites of companies where you would like to work. Most business sites will have a tab for "Careers." Job openings are often listed there first, before they are advertised. Some companies have a place where you can set up a profile or choose what type of job you are interested in. Then the company will notify you if a job becomes available.

If you don't know the web address of the business you want to target, go to a search engine, such as Google, and type in the name. If it is a small company, put in the location as well.

It's important to check websites regularly. When a company posts a job, you want to be one of the first people to apply.

Write a list of employers that you want to target. Who do you want to work for? Choose 10 to 15 companies, and find their websites.

Employer	Contact information & web address

3. **Social media.** You may already have social media accounts, such as Facebook or Twitter. Many companies use social media, too. Sometimes companies post job openings on social media. It's a good idea to follow companies you are interested in on social media to stay up to date about what they are doing as well as to be alerted to any job postings they share.

   LinkedIn (www.linkedin.com) is the main social media site for businesses. This is where professionals network and get to know each other. Many employers post jobs on LinkedIn because they can search profiles and find good workers.

   One great thing about LinkedIn is that you can search job opportunities as well as post your credentials and skills in an online profile that reads like a résumé. You can also join groups that relate to your career direction. For instance, Certified Nursing Assistants (CNAs) have a forum to gather and share their thoughts. Besides searching for job opportunities, you can look for your target employers and their employees. One great way to use LinkedIn is to try to connect with people at companies where positions are posted, so they are more likely to know of you when you apply for a job. To learn more about LinkedIn, visit www.gcflearnfree.org/linkedin.

   Don't spend too much time on social media. One problem is that the internet and social networking can become a time waster. When you visit these websites, set a time limit and define your objectives before you go online. Just like you shouldn't grocery shop without a list when you are hungry, you should not visit a social networking website without a list of goals and objectives. For example, you might plan to spend one hour online, twice a week, checking the LinkedIn profiles for companies on your list. Or you may decide to spend 30 minutes reading Facebook posts to learn more about a company.

You can learn about using LinkedIn at this website.

Exercise: My List of Employment Websites

There are hundreds of employment websites. Not all of them will be right for you or the type of job you are looking for. Spend some time looking at these sites, and think about which ones might be best for you. Choose three to five sites to set up email notifications or check out at least four times a week. If you hear of other sites that worked for friends, you can add them to the list.

Website	What I liked or didn't like about it	How often I will check it
www.indeed.com		
www.simplyhired.com		
My state/city or job center website		
My local newspaper website		
Company website		
www.linkedin.com		

Look offline for job openings.

Remember that most jobs are not found online, but in real life. So, step away from the computer and go meet people. Here are some great ways to meet people who may lead you to a new job.

1. **Volunteer activities.** A great place to find out about opportunities is by volunteering at local programs. Many organizations look for volunteers to do different tasks. Sometimes they will provide training. Find a local **nonprofit** program that you respect, and offer to volunteer some time. First, you will get experience that you can list on your résumé. Second, you will feel good about volunteering and helping other people. Third, you may meet people who could hire you or refer you to someone who has a job opening.

nonprofit – for the purpose of helping society instead of making a profit

When you volunteer, treat your work like it is a paying job. You want your supervisors and co-workers to see what you can offer as an employee. That includes being on time, having a good attitude, dressing professionally, and completing your assigned tasks.

Find a nonprofit organization that does activities related to what you want to do in your work. For example, if you want to be in restaurant work, you may want to volunteer with an organization that prepares food for the homeless or delivers meals to senior citizens, like Meals on Wheels. If you want to work in construction, consider volunteering with Habitat for Humanity, where you can get some home-building experience. If you want to work in health care, check with your local hospital for volunteer opportunities.

Some nonprofit organizations may ask you to go through a volunteer application process. Treat the application process seriously. Nonprofit organizations will check the backgrounds of people who are working with children and doing other important services.

2. Newspaper and magazine "Help Wanted" ads. While more companies post jobs online, you can still find job ads in local newspapers or free community magazines. Often, you will find entry-level jobs that do not require lots of education or experience. While this may not be your dream job, it can be a place to start if you have little work experience. It might also be a way to get a foot in the door with a good company. Often you can move up to another position if you do good work.

You can usually buy a newspaper at your local grocery store or corner market. The Sunday paper is more expensive than the regular paper, but it often has a large section with job ads. Often these same stores will have free community magazines that you can pick up. Also look for articles in the business section that might tell about new companies planning to open in your town. If you know that a restaurant or store is opening soon, you may be able to find job ads on its website before they are printed in the local newspaper.

3. Job fairs. Often, organizations like the chamber of commerce or a local employment center will host a job fair. At job fairs, dozens of local and national companies have booths with representatives who are looking for job candidates. They may be prepared to interview potential candidates.

Job fairs have positives and negatives.

Positives:

- You can meet lots of employers in one place.
- You can practice your elevator speech.
- Employers are serious about hiring.
- There are often many entry-level jobs.

Negatives:

- Not all employers attend job fairs.
- You are competing with lots of other job seekers.
- You may not find the type of employers or jobs that interest you.

With a job fair, you only have a limited amount of time. Before you go, if possible, get a list of employers who are attending. Sometimes one large company holds a job fair if it has many openings. Find out what jobs they are hiring for, and see what openings interest you. Then make a list of booths to visit.

Be prepared for a job fair:

- Dress professionally, as if you are going to an interview.
- Bring several copies of your résumé, including customized résumés and cover letters for specific employers and positions.
- Practice your elevator speech.

The more prepared you are, the better your chances will be for success. Yes, it does require some planning and work. But investing the time will increase your chances for getting an interview or a job.

Write an elevator speech.

Often, you will have just a short time to make your case for being a good employee. For example, you may run into a manager from one of your target companies while you are doing volunteer work. You can't waste the chance to make a connection, but you need to introduce yourself quickly. A short, introduction about who you are and what you do is sometimes called an elevator speech. It should take no more than 30 seconds. In those 30 seconds, state your name, your desired job, your key selling points, and the best reasons for hiring you.

Read this example:

> "Hi, my name is Juan Jobseeker and I am a Certified Nursing Assistant. I would like to work as a home health aide for a company that provides home care to seniors. I have been a CNA since 2009, and I have worked in nursing homes and at a home health care agency. I am skilled in record keeping and have an eye for detail. I really enjoy working with senior citizens. I have strong experience and a solid commitment to helping my elderly clients."

Exercise: My Elevator Speech

On the lines below, write your elevator speech. Practice saying it aloud. Time yourself. Try to keep it shorter than 30 seconds, but don't speak too fast. **Revise** your speech as often as you need to for use with different employers or in different situations. Practice saying it to other students or friends so that you can say it easily and naturally.

revise – look over and change in order to improve something

_____

_____

_____

_____

_____

4. American Job Centers and nonprofit workforce agencies. States and local governments have agencies to help unemployed and **underemployed** workers. Visit your local job center or career one-stop and ask about programs they have to help you find a new job. Job centers often have computers for you to use, and they will have local jobs posted on their boards. They sometimes sponsor job fairs, and they can give you feedback on your résumé. To find a job center near you, visit www.careeronestop.org. Click on "find local help."

    Your community may also have a nonprofit workforce agency, which offers programs to help people find new jobs. Search town and city websites in your area to look for links to workforce agencies. These websites may also have information about open positions and job fairs for local agencies.

5. **Adult education programs**. Are you attending adult education classes? If so, your program probably has a staff member who helps people get ready for work or career training. Make an appointment with that person. He or she can help you find workforce programs in your community. You can also get feedback on your résumé and cover letter. Your program may have an employability class. You can ask the teacher for help. If your program is part of a community college, the college may have a job placement center to help students looking for work. Many people want to help you reach your goals. You just have to ask.

6. **Local businesses.** One more way to find a new job is to go to a company in person to fill out an employment application. This may seem old-fashioned, but many people get jobs this way.

    When you go to apply for a job, dress as if you were going to an interview. Why? Because first impressions are important. Also, you might actually get an interview on the spot, so be prepared. When you are dressed professionally, you will be in the right frame of mind to succeed. Be polite and friendly to everyone when you are at the company. The person sitting at the front desk could be your new boss or the assistant to your new boss.

    Politely ask if you can fill out an employment application. They may give you a form, or they may ask you to fill out the form online. Either way, you can still ask to leave a copy of your résumé. You can also ask to meet with someone from human resources to discuss job opportunities. If you meet the HR manager, be sure to give your elevator speech.

    Bring several copies of your résumé and a notepad and pen to take notes on the job hiring process. Bring any information that you need to complete a job application. (Most of this information should be on your résumé.) Plan on spending anywhere from 30 minutes to one hour completing the application. Smile and greet anyone you see. Everyone you meet is a possible job connection.

underemployed – working at a job that does not meet your needs

You can find a local job center using this website.

Bring this information when you complete a standard job application:

- Your contact information (mailing address and phone numbers)

- Your educational history including dates, school names and locations, degrees and certificates, training courses, etc.

- Your work history including dates, employer names and locations, job titles, and duties

- References (names and contact information)

- Other relevant information such as military history, volunteer history, or salary history

- Two forms of identification such as a driver's license and a Social Security card (at least one ID card should have your photo)

references – people that potential employers can ask about your skills and work ethic

salary – fixed pay for regular work

Fill out applications completely and honestly.

Employers can and will run background checks on possible employees. So be 100% truthful when filling out a job application. Lying on a job application is grounds for termination. Even if you get hired, you can be fired if your employer finds out you lied.

Complete the application as fully as possible. If you leave out information, it can cost you an opportunity. If certain items do not apply to you, you can put "N/A" for "Not Applicable" or "Does not apply" on that section of the application. Try to answer every question.

grounds for termination – reason that a company can fire someone

Follow these tips when filling out a standard job application:

- Read the entire application form before you begin to write.

- Follow all directions completely.

- Do not skip anything.

- If a question is not applicable, write either "Does not apply" or "N/A."

- Answer every question honestly.

- If you would like to explain an answer, write, "Will discuss in the interview."

- If you have a criminal record, answer yes to questions about a criminal history, then, write "Will discuss in the interview." Let the employer know that you are willing to explain the details in person.

- Double check names, dates, telephone numbers, and addresses you write.

Exercise: My Basic Job Application

Fill out the simple job application on page 19. Ask the teacher or a classmate for help when you need it. There is a more detailed application on our website. Fill it out and take it with you when you fill out applications.

Sample Employment/Job Application

For more practice, print out a sample application on our website. You can also fill out the sample online application.

APPLICANT INFORMATION

Last Name	First		M.I.	Date
Street Address			Apartment/Unit #	
City	State		ZIP	
Phone	Email Address			
Date Available	Social Security No.		Desired Salary	
Position Applied for				

EDUCATION

High School		Address	
From To	Did you graduate? YES NO	Degree	
College		Address	
From To	Did you graduate? YES NO	Degree	
Other		Address	
From To	Did you graduate? YES NO	Degree	

PREVIOUS EMPLOYMENT

Please list two previous employers.

Company	Phone	
Address	Supervisor	
Job Title	Starting Date:	Ending Date:
Responsibilities		
Company	Phone	
Address	Supervisor	
Job Title	Starting Date:	Ending Date:
Responsibilities		

REFERENCES

Please list two professional references.

Full Name	Relationship
Company	Phone
Address	
Full Name	Relationship
Company	Phone
Address	

You can also practice filling out a sample online job application on our website. You can fill out online job applications either by typing in the information or by cutting and pasting the information from another document into an online application.

Lesson 3   Networking Your Way to a Job

What is networking? Networking is reaching out to people to get information or to share ideas. You can network with people you know, such as friends, family, co-workers, and others. Or you can try to meet new people who do the kind of work you want to do or who work at a place you'd like to work. The goal of networking is to help you reach your goal—to get a job.

With a job search, the goal of networking is usually to get introduced to someone who can hire you. Many people think that networking only applies to the job search. However, networking helps with many needs in life. For instance, have you ever asked a friend for the name of a good doctor? That is networking. When you network, you **exchange** information with someone who has a common interest.

exchange – give something and receive something in return

You may not realize how many people you know who can help you in your job search. Likely, you know several people who can help you find a new job. That does not mean that they can hire you, but they may be able to help you find someone who will hire you. When you network, ask for help, not for a job.

Networking is the most effective way to find a new job.

There is a saying, "It's not *what* you know, it's *who* you know." This saying is true when you're looking for a job. There is no shame in using contacts and relationships to find a job. In fact, it's the smart way to search for a job.

Become a best-known candidate.

When employers have an open position, they go through a hiring process like the one you read about in Lesson 1. Hiring managers will first look at their list of best-known candidates. These are good, potential employees they already know and trust. How do you become a best-known candidate? One way is through a referral from someone in your network.

For example, if you did a good job when you volunteered your time to cook meals for a shelter, the manager there might tell a friend who owns a restaurant about you. If the restaurant owner is curious about you, she might look for you on LinkedIn. If your LinkedIn profile shows the experience you have as a cook, that experience may be a good fit for the restaurant. When the restaurant owner needs a new cook, she may think of you. Now you are on the list of best-known candidates!

Regardless of your background, you would be surprised at the people you know who can help you. Think about the contacts you already have. Check your list in Lesson 1. One great thing about networking is that you don't even have to know the people who will hire you. It could be a friend of a friend or someone who heard about you from a previous employer.

Learn how to network.

Networking is a process. It takes practice to network successfully. There are five key steps to successful networking:

1. Commit to networking
2. Inventory your contacts
3. Start with people you know
4. Use LinkedIn when appropriate
5. Conduct informational interviews

appropriate – right or proper for the situation

Commit to networking.

Successful networking requires a strong commitment. At times, networking can be scary and frustrating. You also need to be patient. Networking takes time and hard work, and it may seem easier to search for jobs online. However, people find more jobs through networking than searching online ads.

frustrating – causing feelings of anger and annoyance

Here are some tips:

- Let people know that you are looking for a new job. Set goals for how many people you want to contact. A good goal would be to network with at least five people each week. Contact friends, family members, classmates, co-workers, etc.

- Get as much information as you can from others. When you talk to people, ask for their ideas for your job search. Try to find out which companies and industries are hiring. Get ideas on where to look and how you should talk to people who can help you. If a friend talks about how much he likes his job, find out where he works. Ask lots of questions.

- Get referrals. Ask each person you meet for the name of at least one additional contact. Use your contacts to make new contacts.

- Focus on potential employers. Try to meet people from the list of companies you want to target. Think about where you might see people who work at the companies. Are there stores or restaurants nearby? Are there local clubs they might belong to?

- Avoid asking people for a job. That will make them feel uncomfortable and they may be less willing to talk with you. You want to ask for information, try to get them to talk about their jobs or employers.

- Give something back to your network. Help is not a one-way street. Think of information or other help you can offer people who help you. Maybe you have ideas or contacts to help them. Maybe you know someone who could be a potential customer. People are more likely to help you if you offer to help them in some way.

- Clearly communicate your value as an employee. Your elevator speech will give you some points to share when networking. Talk about what you can offer. Focus on the positive.

Here are some tools you should create for networking:

1. **Exit Statement.** When you network with people, they may ask why you are looking for a job. An exit statement is a brief explanation of why you left a job. If you are working on your high school credential or attending a certification program, prepare a short statement on why you chose that program and what career you are pursuing. Focus on the future. Give your networking contacts enough information to share with others who may be able to help you.

If you were laid off from your last job, briefly explain why it didn't work out. Be honest, but don't go into detail. If you are looking for your first job, briefly explain why you haven't worked before. For example, "I've been caring for my children, but now I am ready to enter the workforce." Or, "I took some time to concentrate on getting my diploma. Now I am focusing on my career." Whatever your situation, give a brief reason on why you are searching for a job. Make your exit message as positive and upbeat as possible.

2. **Job Search Mission Statement.** The second thing your contact needs to know is what type of job you want to get. Your job search mission statement should include the type of job you are seeking, the type of employer you are targeting, and the location you want to work. If you read *WorkWise: Choosing a Job*, you already wrote your mission statement. Re-read it, and make revisions if anything has changed. If you don't have a mission statement, write one. Here is a frame you can use:

My mission is to obtain a _____ position with a _____ that is _____.

3. **Business Cards and Résumés.** The third thing people will need is your contact information. They may also ask for your résumé. Business cards are easy to hand to your networking contacts. On the back of the card, you can print details of your qualifications or your elevator speech. You can create business cards on a computer program like Microsoft Publisher or Microsoft Word, or an office supply store can help you make cards. Here is a sample job seeker business card:

Juan Jobseeker Jr.	**Juan Jobseeker Jr.**
Seeking	Certified Nursing Assistant seeking home health aide position to provide home care to seniors.
CNA/Home Health Aide Position	• CNA certificate, Dallas Nursing School, 2009
555-123-4567/555-765-4321	• Experience in nursing homes and in home health care
juan.jobseeker@email.com	• Skill in recordkeeping, eye for detail
www.linkedin.com/in/juan-jobseeker	• Enjoy working with seniors
	• Committed to working with home clients
Front	Back

4. **Target List of Employers.** Another question you may hear while networking is, "Where do you want to work?" Prepare a list of at least 10 prospective employers that would be ideal for you. Choose employers in your area that hire for the position you are seeking and that need employees with your skills.

5. **Networking Handbill.** One more tool you might choose to use for networking is a handbill or flyer. This is a one-page summary of who you are and what you are looking for. Your handbill describes where you want to go and what you can do. Your networking handbill should have a brief profile, possible titles or positions, and a list of target companies. Most importantly, it should have a **value proposition**, which tells the value you bring as an employee. You can also make customized versions for job fairs or prospective employers.

value proposition – statement that sums up who you are and why you would be an asset to a company that hires you

Sample Networking Handbill

Juan Jobseeker Jr.

1234 Your Street, Apt. 432, Dallas, TX 75205
Home: 555-123-4567 / Cell: 555-765-4321
juan.jobseeker@email.com
www.linkedin.com/in/juan-jobseeker

Professional Objective:
Certified Nursing Assistant/Home Health Aide for Home Health Care Company
Seeking a position where I can use my experience, attention to detail, and customer service skills to assist senior citizens and help them safely stay longer in their homes.

Preferred Positions:
- In Home Nurse Assistant
- Home Health Aide

Value Proposition:
Detail-oriented CNA with strong recordkeeping skills. Able to maintain strong client satisfaction while helping senior citizens with daily living activities so they can stay in their homes. Guaranteed high customer satisfaction and quality service.

Target Area:
- *Geography:* Greater Dallas/Ft. Worth, TX area
- *Industries:* Health care
- *Type of Employer:* Small or medium sized company providing in-home assistance for senior citizens and other clients

Target List of Employers:
- Home Angels Service
- Super Great Home Healthcare
- Dallas Hospital Home Healthcare
- Ft. Worth Home Healthcare
- North Dallas Home
- True Heart Home Health Agency
- Bright Haven Home Health, LLC

Complete this handbill for yourself.

Name

Address

Phone number(s)

Email address

LinkedIn profile address

Professional Objective

Preferred Positions

- _____

- _____

- _____

Value Proposition

Target Area

- Geography: _____

- Industries: _____

- Type of Employer: _____

Target List of Employers:

- _____

- _____

- _____

- _____

- _____

- _____

Inventory your contacts.

You probably know many people who can give you valuable information as you network. Now think about the people you know. When you **inventory** your contacts, you will make a complete list of everyone you know who can help with your job search. Make notes about where they work and what they can help with. These details can make your networking list stronger. In Lesson 1, you made a starter list. Now, do some more thinking and add to your networking list.

Start by listing family and friends, then add former co-workers, former bosses, former customers, current and former teachers, and other adult education students. In addition, think about fellow members of your place of worship and community organizations. Also, you can ask people like your barber or hair stylist, doctor, or other business owners you know.

Your hair stylists and doctors all have many clients. If you are lucky, some of these clients might know a businessperson who could use an employee like you. You might be thinking, "Why would I talk to a hair stylist or a barber?" Business owners, hiring managers, and HR managers all need to get their hair cut too. Usually when getting haircuts, people like to talk. They may mention that they need to hire someone. You never know where or when an opportunity might come up.

Here is a list of people to get you started. You may want to add these potential network contacts to your list:

- Clergy members

- Family

- Friends

- Students you know from school, training classes, or certification programs

- Former (and/or current) co-workers

- Former (and/or current) bosses

- Former (and/or current) customers, vendors, and suppliers

- Former (and/or current) teachers

- Doctors, dentists

- Hair stylists or barbers

- Members of your churches or synagogues

- Fellow volunteers for a nonprofit organization

- Fellow members of community organizations

inventory – count and record

Potential places to network include:

- Community meetings
- Charity events or fundraisers
- Employment centers or career transition centers
- State and nonprofit workforce agencies
- Political organizations
- Chambers of commerce
- Parent-teacher meetings or other school events
- Holiday parties
- Children's activities or events

Exercise: My Bigger Networking List

You may not think you know anyone who can help in your job search, but as your list grows, you may be surprised. Check the list you made in Lesson 1. Now, think of people from your community, your place of worship, your neighborhood, your friends, and your teachers. Read through the above lists and think carefully. List at least 10 more people who you will ask for job search advice.

_____   _____

_____   _____

_____   _____

_____   _____

_____   _____

You now have an even bigger list of networking contacts. Your list will continue to grow!

Start with the people you know.

Now it is time to start planning how to contact the people you know on your networking list.

The people on your networking list probably fall into one of these four categories:

- **Informal acquaintances.** Informal acquaintances are people you have met, but you do not know well. You probably know a little about them or you have something in common. A neighbor on your block or a fellow volunteer in an organization may be an acquaintance. However, you can get to know them better.

- **Possible allies.** Possible allies are people you know somewhat well. These people respect you, and you respect them. Allies will speak highly of you, but may not do much more than that. Again, if you spend time with them, you can get to know them better.

- **Job search advocates.** Advocates are people who not only think highly of you, they will actively try to help you get a new job. These could be close friends, former co-workers, former bosses, or teachers. Former co-workers and bosses can be the best advocates because they know your skills and the quality of your work. They will speak up for you. If you have the right skills and experience that an employer needs, these people will likely watch for job openings for you. You want to spend most of your networking time with this group of people.

- **Negative time-wasters.** Negative time-wasters are people who just like to complain or who enjoy other people's misery. Some people try to make themselves look good by tearing other people down. Avoid negative time-wasters while networking. They will suck up your time and drain your energy. When you meet people like this, politely thank them for their help, and move on.

Spend your time wisely. Spend most of your networking efforts focusing on people who are allies or advocates. Ideally, you want a few great advocates working on your behalf. Be sure you give these contacts all the tools you have to help you succeed.

Use your networking tools. Your marketing tools can include résumés, business cards, and networking handbills. Use your elevator speech to describe the job you want when you speak with your contacts. Give your handbills and business cards to people in your network so they can recommend you.

When contacting your network for the first time, clearly express your goals.

It's best to write out a script and practice saying it. That way you won't forget anything important. Your script should clearly state exactly what you would like your contact to help you with. Here is a sample networking script:

> *"Hi Robert, this is Jane Candidate. How are you? I know it has been a while since we talked. I am currently looking for a job in the hospitality field. I am reaching out to you because I respect your opinion. I was wondering if I could get your feedback on the plan I have put together for my job search."*

Meet in person. While it takes time, you will have better success meeting with your contacts face to face. When you meet, your contacts may not offer help right away. Don't worry. Tell them what you need, and let them think it over. People will remember ideas later. Every few weeks, call the people who are your best advocates and allies. Say something like, "Have you had a chance to look at the companies I'm interested in? I was wondering if you came up with any names of people I might contact."

Use LinkedIn when appropriate.

You can also make connections on LinkedIn, and find new contacts to add to your network. One way to build your LinkedIn network is by joining groups. If you want to work in hospitality, search for groups that focus on the hospitality industry, and join a group that relates to the type of job you want. This is a great way to make new contacts and to begin networking with decision-makers. You can also look up and follow companies that you'd like to work for.

Invite your face-to-face contacts to be part of your LinkedIn network. If they are active on LinkedIn, they may be able to introduce you to other contacts. Reach out to your social connections. They may not be close friends, but don't ignore them. You can also connect with people from community organizations or other groups in your area. Some of these people might have good business connections or contacts in your field. When you meet new contacts in person, invite them to connect on LinkedIn.

Remember, in addition to asking for help on LinkedIn, you should help others when you can. If you help people when they need it, they will be more likely to help you.

When you invite someone to be part of your network, send a note to make the invitation more personal. LinkedIn can be a big help, but don't forget to do most of your networking in person. Don't let LinkedIn replace your face-to-face meetings!

Conduct informational interviews.

Earlier, we talked about how informational interviews can help you. When you are networking, you will conduct many informational interviews. Always make a list of questions before you meet with someone. Some questions will be the same for everyone, but you may want to add some questions that are tailored to each person you meet. Here are some sample questions that you may want to ask:

- Could you please tell me a little about your background and how you came to work for _____?

- What do you find interesting about your work?

- What do you like most about your job?

- What do you like least about your job?

- What background and education are needed to work in your field?

- What is the best way to find opportunities in this field?

- May I give you a little background on myself? I would like to know if you think my experience and education make me a good fit in your field?

- If you were me, how would you explore opportunities in this field?

- Do you know any people in the field that I should introduce myself to?

open-ended questions – questions that call for more than yes, no, or one-word answers

Choose the questions that most help you. Make the most of this time to learn new things. You may also think of your own questions. Networking is a fine art. If you ask, "Do you know of any jobs?" people may just say no. However, if you ask **open-ended questions** and show a positive attitude, people may be willing to open up and talk more. You want your contacts to know you and care about you, so they will want to help you. Having a good, productive conversation can set the right tone. You want people to remember you fondly and recommend you if they hear about a job opening in your field.

<u>**Exercise: My Networking Plan**</u>

On the lines below, make a starter networking plan for yourself. Give yourself deadlines.

Networking Activity	How I plan to do this	When/where I plan to do this
Hand out business cards		
Hand out networking handbills		
Informational interview 1		
Informational interview 2		
Informational interview 3		
Informational interview 4		
Informational interview 5		

Do not stop networking after just five informational interviews. Your goal should be to network with at least five people a week. Keep networking until you reach your goal!

Now get started!

With your tools, it is now time to get started. At first networking may seem to be a bit scary, but keep at it. Start with people you already know and care about you. As you keep networking, at some point, you will become a "best-known candidate" and be ahead of the competition for a new job.

determine – decide

After networking and sending out dozens of résumés, you finally get an interview. Now is an important time. Your interview will **determine** whether you get the job. Therefore, you must prepare carefully and be ready. A sports team practices hard before a big game. An actor rehearses hundreds of times before starring in a play. Your interview is like the big game or the opening night—and you need to practice and prepare in order to do well.

In this unit, you will learn about

- Positioning Yourself for Success (Lesson 4)

- Responding to Interview Questions and Objections (Lesson 5)

- Taking Care of Details (Lesson 6).

Of all the steps involved in the job search, few are more important than preparing for job interviews. Plan to spend at least one day preparing for each hour of an interview. How should you practice? This unit will show how to answer common, difficult job interview questions. In addition, you will learn how to overcome objections that can make the difference in getting hired or not. This unit will show you how to practice and what you need to ace your interviews and get a new job!

Self-Check: What do I know about job interviews?

Have you ever gone to a job interview? What do you think happens in an interview?

_____

_____

_____

_____

What happened at your last job interview?

_____

_____

What worries you most about job interviews?

_____

_____

After you work through lessons 4, 5, and 6, review your answers again. What have you learned about interviews that will help you? Are you less worried about job interviews now?

Lesson 4   Positioning Yourself for Success

How do you position yourself for success? You prepare yourself well for the interview so you can clearly present your value as an employee. Showing interviewers that you are a valuable employee will make them want to hire you. To do your best at a job interview, you need to spend time and energy getting ready. Here are some tips to help you position yourself for success at your next interview.

Research the company before the interview.

Before your interview, research the company, so you can understand the employees and what they do, and the job you are applying for. Many candidates skip this important step. Today, information is at your fingertips. The best place to start researching a company is on the internet. Locate the company website and look for the "About" section. This will give you an overview of what the company does. You can also look for the employer's LinkedIn page, Facebook page, and Twitter feed.

What should you look for when you research an employer? Here are some important points you should learn about in your research.

- **Mission Statement.** Most companies and organizations have mission statements that explain their purpose. The mission statement will tell you what the company cares deeply about. Sometimes the meaning will be very clear, using words like, "Our mission is . . ." Or you may need to **infer** their mission. A company may say, "We provide a high quality dining experience at a reasonable price." That means their mission is to give their customers great food and service that's affordable. Look for a statement that tells what is important to the company.

  infer – make a reasonable guess about something based on facts

  Small businesses have a mission, even if they have not stated it. You can infer this from their main product or service. For example, a construction company may only build fast-food restaurants. You can infer that the mission of the company is to build fast-food restaurants that fit the requirements and schedules of the fast food chains it works with.

  The mission statement can tell you about a company's values and beliefs. Print a copy of the mission statement for each company you interview with. When preparing for your job interview, think about how you can help the company achieve its mission. (You may be asked this during the interview.) Then, come up with several key selling points that show how you will help the company achieve its mission.

  For example, with the restaurant mentioned above, you could talk about your customer service ability or your excellent cooking skills. With the construction company, you could emphasize your ability to carefully follow plans and to work as part of a team to get a task done on time.

  In the interview, if you can talk about exactly how you intend to help an organization achieve its mission, you will increase your chances for success.

- **Products and Services.** The next item to research is the company or organization's main business. What products do they offer? What services do they provide? Think about who does business with the company and why. Does the store sell inexpensive items or high price items? Does the restaurant serve fast food or elegant meals? What are the most popular items? Why? Ask yourself questions about the potential employer so you will understand the company's needs better. That way you can talk more knowledgably about how you can help.

- **Customers and Clients.** The terms "customers" and "clients" may seem the same. However, customers usually purchase the goods a business sells, and clients are customers that a business has an ongoing relationship with. A business might work with a client to sell goods that are customized for that client. For example, people who buy a meal from a restaurant or items from a store are customers. A senior citizen who hires a home health company to provide assistance in her home is a client.

  Try to understand what a company's clients or customers expect. For example, a fast-food customer wants to get meals quickly. Meanwhile, a home health client will want people to talk with her and get to know her personal needs. Consider how you can use your skills or **qualities** help a company serve its customers or clients well.

- **Competition.** Most of your targeted employers will have competition, and you need to learn as much as you can about them. Learning about the competition will help you in the following ways. First, the more you understand the competition, the better you can think of ways to help your future employer beat the competition. Second, the more you learn about a company's competition, the more you will expand your own opportunities. If the interview doesn't work out, but you really liked the industry, you can look for opportunities at competitors.

Job hunters who research the companies they interview with usually get more job offers. So, the research is worth the time and effort.

Exercise: Research My Target Company

By now, you have a list of target companies. Pick one. Research the company and write the information on the lines below.

Name of Company

_____

Website Address

_____

Mission Statement

_____

_____

qualities – noticeable features of someone or something

Products/Services

Clients/Customers

Competition

Research your interviewers.

Along with researching the company, try to find out what you can about the people who will interview you. If you know the name of the interviewer, you can probably find some information on LinkedIn. If you do not know the name, look on the company website to see if the names of key employees are listed. You may be able to find the name of the HR manager or the head of the department you are applying for.

Check the Facebook and LinkedIn company profiles. You can also do a search for the company or search for news articles about the company. Often the names of key employees appear in news items about businesses. The more you know about your interviewer, the easier it will be to talk to him or her.

After you find the names of people who may interview you, search for their LinkedIn profiles. Review their background, job history, accomplishments, and interests. Do you have anything in common? Look for a photo, so you can recognize the interviewer when you get there. If the interviewer does not have a LinkedIn page, check Facebook and Google.

Look for relevant topics to talk about. For example, if you find out the interviewer volunteers for a nonprofit organization you support, mention the organization during the interview. Look for ways to get the interviewer to talk about himself so that you can learn more about him and the company. The interviewer will be impressed if you make an effort to learn about the company.

And remember, the interviewer may also be looking for information about you.

Exercise: What I Have in Common With an Interviewer

When you meet an interviewer, you want to understand him or her as much as you can. Keep in mind that interviewers are people too. An interview will go well if you get along with the interviewer and discuss things you have in common.

Imagine that you have an interview with Rick Scott. He used to be a lawyer, but he always loved cooking, so he started a restaurant. Along with running his business, Rick has three kids, two from a marriage that ended in divorce, and one with his current wife. When Rick is not busy at the restaurant, he enjoys watching the local football and basketball teams. Rick lives in your hometown. He also went to school there. Rick volunteers with Meals on Wheels and regularly contributes food to the local homeless shelter.

You may be nervous about meeting Rick for the interview. But you and Rick probably have some things in common. Fill out this diagram to show what things you and the interviewer have in common.

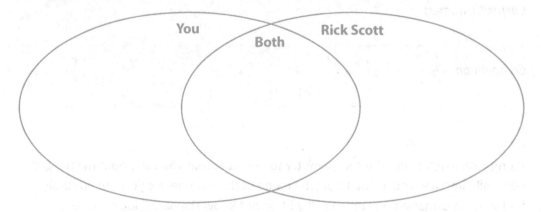

Decide what questions to ask.

The next step in positioning yourself for success is to list questions to ask the interviewer. Though you should be prepared to answer the interviewer's questions, you can also ask questions. In fact, most interviewers will expect you to have questions. This is your opportunity to find out more about the company and the job opening. If you do not have thoughtful questions, the interviewer may think you are not really interested in the job. Plan your questions carefully.

Interviewing can be a little like dating. If you ask too many questions or the wrong questions, then the interview may not go very well. Ask questions that prove that you already know a little about the company. Show that you are confident in your knowledge and abilities by asking thought-provoking and strong questions about the job or the company.

The key is to ask the right questions at the right time. For instance, when you first meet an interviewer, don't ask, "What are your benefits? or "How much vacation time will I get?" This will make you sound like you are not a hard worker and you are not serious about the job. Save these questions for later—at a second interview or after you get a job offer.

An important question to ask is "Can you describe the ideal candidate for this position?" Listen to the interviewer, and find out what is important to him or her. Then try to show through your answers and conversation how you fit the interviewer's idea of the ideal candidate. If the interviewer describes someone very different from you, you probably won't get the job. Not every job will be the right fit for you. Be honest and act professionally. Maybe the company will have another opening that is more suited to you.

Ask open-ended questions to get the interviewer to talk and give thoughtful responses. When you research a company, write down any questions that come up. Before the interview, ask yourself these questions and take notes.

- What questions can I ask to learn more about the job?

- What questions will help me know how the company decides who gets the job?

- What can I ask that will get the interviewer talk more about the company?

- What questions do I want to ask at the end to find out about the next steps?

Meanwhile, here are some open-ended questions that you may want to ask at the interview. Do not try to ask all these questions. Pick a few that make the most sense for your interview, and write them down.

- Can you describe the ideal candidate for this position?

- What do you see as the keys to success in this job?

- What are the most important responsibilities of this position?

- Tell me about your team members and how you see me working with them?

- In this job, who would I report to?

- What type of support is available for a person in this job?

- How often do you have employee reviews? Can you describe the process?

- In general, what types of decisions would I be expected to make without guidance? What decisions would I discuss with my supervisor?"

- This is an exciting opportunity, and we seem to understand each other. I think I would be a great member of your team. What is the next step in this process?

- It would be an honor to be part of your team. If you decide to hire me, how quickly would I be able to start?

- What is your target start date for this position?

Questions show your interest, thoughts, and preparation. Asking questions not only demonstrates your ability to listen, but also shows you are ready to work hard and succeed. Write down the questions you want to ask and bring this list with you to the interview. Bringing notes will make you look like you are well-prepared. And take notes during the interview so you'll remember what is said.

Exercise: My Starter List of Questions to Ask Interviewers

Make list of at least five open-ended questions to ask at an interview. Check the list above. Write questions that will help you to find out about the company, the position, and how the company chooses employees.

_____

_____

_____

_____

_____

_____

Bring printed items to leave behind.

When professional salespeople meet with clients, they often leave some printed material behind. For example, they may leave a brochure of products to remind the client what they talked about. When you leave something with the interviewer, you increase the chances that he or she will remember you. Here are a few suggestions for what to leave behind.

- **Résumé:** Bring a copy of your résumé to leave with the interviewer. Even if you already sent your résumé to the company, bring along printed copies. Hand one to each person you meet with at the interview. Bring several copies, just in case you are introduced to more people. Customize your résumé to the job, so everyone will see that you are a good fit.

- **Letters of recommendation:** Sometimes, if you leave a job on good terms, your boss offers to write a letter of recommendation. This is a letter that tells about why you are a good employee. Sometimes a customer writes to thank you for good service. Or a teacher may write a letter saying that you are a dedicated student. Do you have any letters of recommendation from previous coworkers, clients, suppliers, or professors? If so, make copies of these letters and attach them to the résumés you bring. If you know someone who might write a letter of recommendation for you, don't be afraid to ask.

- **Personal business cards:** If you have personal business cards, bring them with you. Hand one to each person you meet. The cards make it is easy to contact you.

- **Networking handbill:** Customize your networking handbill to the employer and position. Remove the list of targeted companies. Add in some key selling points that you think will be important to the company. Highlight any specific experience or skills that make you a good candidate for the job.

Lesson 5   Responding to Interview Questions and Objections

There is an old saying that practice makes perfect. In a sense, your interview is like a performance, and rehearsing will help you perform at your best.

Prepare for your interviews by practicing answers to common questions and objections you are most likely to face. Objections are reasons the interviewer might use to say you are not fit for the job. In this lesson, you will learn some typical job interview questions and objections. The more you learn about these, the better prepared you will be.

objection – argument against something

Use notecards to prepare.

On each notecard, write a common question. Try to write at least 20 questions. Put the notecards in a large bowl. Ask a family member or friend to act as the interviewer and pick a question from the bowl and read it. Answer the question just as if you were in an interview. Practice answering all the questions. You can also use this same exercise to practice responding to possible objections.

You can also use the worksheets available on our website. There are 48 practice interview questions and 12 practice objections. You can print them and cut them out like notecards.

You can print out the interview questions and objections worksheets on our website.

You cannot predict what questions or objections might come up or in what order. By having someone randomly pick questions and objections out of a bowl, you will get some practice with lots of different possibilities.

Make this exercise like a dress rehearsal. Put on business attire. Prepare a place for the interview—you can use a table or desk with one chair on either side. Greet your "interviewer" and shake hands. Sit down, and then spend about 30 to 45 minutes asking and answering questions. Repeat this rehearsal several times in the week before your interview.

dress rehearsal – final rehearsal before a live show

If you are very nervous about rehearsing with a friend or family member, practice alone first. Read a question out loud, and then practice answering it in front of a mirror.

Practice whenever and wherever possible.

It's not enough to practice saying the answers in your head. In a real interview, you need to speak confidently and clearly. So make your job interview practice as real as possible by speaking aloud. Ask yourself each interview question aloud and give each answer aloud.

If you make a mistake in practice, just keep going. In the real interview, you will need to keep going. If you make a mistake, stay calm. Take a breath, apologize, and continue. After your practice, you can review your performance and think about what went well and what you can improve. If you practice with someone, ask that person for feedback. Tell him or her not to worry about hurting your feelings. You need real feedback to help you prepare for the actual job interview. Work on correcting the things that do not go well in practice.

Be prepared to answer five types of interview questions.

You may be asked all kinds of questions during an interview, but five common types are personality, positional, **mindset**, problem-solving, and career-related questions. Each type of question has a purpose. Understanding the purpose of each question will help you prepare your answer.

mindset – way of thinking

1. **Personality questions.** Employers want to know about a candidate's personality. It's important that managers hire people who will get along well with their team. This is another reason to ask the interviewer to describe the ideal candidate. You might find out what personality traits the company looks for in its employees.

   "Tell me about yourself." This is the most common personality question, and it makes most people nervous. There's no reason to be nervous if you prepare a careful answer. Understand that the interviewer does not want to hear your life story. Actually, he or she wants to find out what you would be like as an employee and if you would be a good fit for team.

   Come up with a short and to-the-point answer. Your answer should be 30 to 60 seconds long. Also, use as many keywords from the job description as you can.

   For example, imagine that you are interviewing to be a server for a fancy restaurant. Some keywords in the job description are *excellent customer service* and *people person*. Your response should describe your outgoing, friendly personality and show that you take pride in giving good service. Look at the sample answer below:

   > *"I have five years of experience working in different restaurants, both as a hostess and as a server. I often get positive reviews from my boss and the customers for my excellent customer service. Some repeat customers ask to sit in my section because they prefer to have me wait on them. I am a people person. I get along well with most people, and I can easily remember customers' names and their favorite foods."*

This answer quickly and effectively shows that the candidate is an excellent server, is friendly and gets along with customers, and cares about customer service. This is what the employer wants to know, and this is the type of person he wants to hire.

38   Preparing for Interviews

© New Readers Press. All rights reserved.

Exercise: What About Me?

Write your response to the prompt, "Tell me about yourself." Your answer should be about four to six sentences, so you can say it in less than one minute. Your answer should describe how your personality fits the job so the employer will know what you are like as an employee. Your elevator speech can give you some ideas for answering this question. You may also check your résumé or a job description for ideas. Keep in mind that you will customize this answer for each job, to suit the employer's needs.

_____

_____

_____

_____

_____

Here are some other personality questions you may be asked:

- "What are your greatest strengths?" In response to this, mention your qualities and skills that relate to the job. Think about the position. What qualities and skills does a person need to do well in this job? Which of those qualities and skills do you have? Highlight your strongest skills in your answer.

- "What is your greatest weakness?" This is tricky. The best response is to mention something that you are working on improving or to talk about a weakness that you have overcome. This helps to show that you have a positive attitude and that you have a desire to learn. For example, "I am not crazy about paperwork, but I know it is important. I took a bookkeeping class to improve my skills, and I work hard at keeping up with it."

2. Positional questions. Interviewers often ask positional questions to see if you have the skills and knowledge to do the job. Here is an example of a positional question, "Why do you feel you are qualified for this position?" The interviewer is looking for what skills and experience make you qualified for the position. If you have asked the interviewer to describe the ideal candidate, then you could talk about your skills and qualities that match the ideal candidate's.

Back up your answer with examples. Look at these two sample answers from the restaurant server:

A. "Well, I have worked at several restaurants, and I know what I am doing."

B. "I have an excellent track record of giving great customer service in restaurants. At Supreme Diner, in just 14 months, I helped increase our Yelp customer satisfaction ratings from an average of three stars to four and a half stars. Each night, I managed 20 tables. And I had 10 regular customers request to be seated in my section every Saturday."

Which is the better answer? Answer A lacks facts and details. Answer B gives clear, specific examples that show that the person is good at her work. When you can, use numbers—like in this example—to show concrete examples of how much work you did or how much something improved.

Another positional question might be, "Why do you want this job?" Be careful answering this question. Do not respond that you need to pay your bills, even if you do! Give an answer that shows that you really want to work with this company. Consider this example:

> *"I want to work with Upscale Bistro because it is a high-quality restaurant with an excellent reputation. This job is a perfect fit for me because I share your passion for providing an elegant dining experience. I would be honored to be part of your team!"*

This answer shows enthusiasm for the company and the position.

3. **Mindset questions.** With these questions, interviewers want to know how your mind works and how you would fit with the rest of the workers at the company. Here are some sample questions and answers.

"How do you like to be managed?" With this question, you want to show that you can work as part of the team. Try a response that shows you care about doing things right, but you do not need constant attention.

> *"I am good at working independently, but I do want to check in with my manager and other team members on a regular basis. This way, I can make sure I am doing what is needed."*

"What management styles do you not like?" Again, you want to be careful. Try to answer in a way that fits what you have learned about the position. The interviewer may be trying to test if there is a style you don't get along with, so it's best to say that you are flexible.

> *"I like getting a lot of feedback, but I understand managers may not always have time to give feedback. So, I am flexible and know how to work well with different management styles."*

"Do you have questions for me?" If you have prepared your questions, you will be ready. Check Lesson 4 for good questions to ask employers. Remember, to save questions about benefits until later in the hiring process.

4. **Problem-solving questions.** With these questions, interviewers want to see how you deal with difficult situations. Here is an example, "Can you tell me about a major challenge you had and how you overcame it?" This questions can be difficult, but you can answer it using the STAR approach.

STAR = **S**ituation + **T**ask + **A**ction + **R**esult

STAR is a technique for answering tough interview questions. Here is an example of how STAR can help you answer the question above about solving a major challenge.

Situation. Describe something a challenge or problem that occurred in your career or your life. Describe the situation by explaining what happened, who was involved, when, where, and how.

> *"Last year, I was a crew leader for a construction project to build a coffee shop. We had five people on the team. Each of us had jobs to do to get this coffee shop built. However, one person was not getting his work done."*

Task. Explain your role in the situation and what task needed to be done. This may be an opportunity to show how you learned or improved a skill.

> *"Somebody on the team needed to talk with this person because without him, we would fall behind schedule. As crew leader, I knew I needed to be the one to talk with this guy and fix the problem."*

Actions. Actions are the steps you took to fix the problem. By explaining your steps, you can show your problem-solving skills.

> *"I went to my team member and spoke to him in private. I told him that the team was worried about staying on schedule and that we needed his help. I asked how I could help him get back on track. He told me that he was having a hard time because some of his tools were stolen just before he started this job. So I found some tools for him to borrow until he could get new ones."*

Results. Tell what happened because of your actions.

> *"After he got the tools, this crew member went to work. He not only completed all of his jobs, he also helped one of the other guys to finish his part. We got the coffee shop built ahead of schedule. I learned that we should not jump to conclusions. It's best to talk to people and face problems head-on. Here, the team and I thought this guy was being lazy. But, he just needed some tools and was embarrassed that his had been stolen."*

Exercise: My STAR Story

Think about a challenge that have you dealt with in the past. Use STAR to describe your challenge.

Situation _____

Task _____

Action _____

Result _____

Sometimes an employer will ask you a problem-solving question about what you would do in a specific situation. Often those questions are about problems that commonly show up in the job or the company. You can also use STAR for those questions.

You can print out the STAR worksheet on our website.

5. **Questions related to your career choice.** Often, interviewers will ask questions related to the position or the field. These questions help the interviewer figure out how much you know about the job. The hiring manager may want to find out how you would handle a common problem on the job. As part of your preparation, search the internet for interview questions for your field. For example, if you want to work as a Certified Nursing Assistant, go to a search engine, such as Google, and type in, "interview questions for Certified Nursing Assistants." Check two or three websites and make a list of common questions. You can also check this site www.readyprepinterview.com and search for the position.

Write answers to the sample questions and practice reading the answers. Or you can use the dress rehearsal activity. Write the questions on cards and have a friend ask you the questions. Practice giving your answers out loud.

You can find job-specific interview questions at this website.

Practice to overcome objections.

An objection is a potential issue or concern that the interviewer may have about hiring you. The interviewer may mention objections about your level of experience, your background, or your education, among other things.

When this happens, remember two things:

1. Keep calm. An objection is not personal. The interviewer is trying hard to find the right person for the job. Interviewers are usually hiring managers. The sooner they fill the position, the sooner they can get back to work. So, in most cases, the interviewer is hoping that you will be the right fit for the job. Practice answering objections before the interview so you will be ready.

2. Objections can be a good sign. If an interviewer has no interest at all, he or she probably won't mention objections. However, if an interviewer does express objections, it may mean he or she is seriously considering hiring you.

Follow these three tips to handle objections.

First, respond positively. Don't start arguing. Instead, you could say, "I understand your feelings. If I were in your position, I would feel the same way." This shows that you can look at things from another person's point of view.

Second, turn what seems to be a negative into a positive. For example, an interviewer may say that you do not have much experience. Try to find a way to focus on the positive: "I understand how you could see it that way. However, while I do not have much experience yet, I have learned a lot in preparing for this career. I have demonstrated my skills in class and during my internship. I have a strong work ethic and I learn quickly. I am sure I could quickly learn your procedures and become a valuable member of your team."

work ethic – commitment to doing one's job well

Third, confirm that you answered the objection. The final step in handling objections is to confirm that you overcame the objection. Avoid using the words "concern" or "objection" when confirming. Instead, you just want to say something simple like, "What are your thoughts?"

Answer honestly and carefully. Understand that the employer is trying to do his or her best to hire the right person. Do your best to show that you are the right person.

Likely, you already have some ideas of objections that interviewers may mention. Plan ahead how you will address them calmly and positively. If you have a criminal record, be prepared to answer that objection. It's best to prepare a short, honest, and positive response. Talk with a re-entry coach or other job counselor to plan your response.

Here are some common objections:

- You don't have enough experience; you are under-qualified.

- You haven't done this job before.

- You haven't worked with clients like this before.

- You did not stay in high school, so I am not sure you will stay with the job.

- You have not had a job for a long time.

Exercise: My Responses to Objections

Think about two or three potential objections that an employer might have about you. Look at the objections worksheet for ideas. Write a response to each objection. Keep your answers short, honest, and positive. Share your responses with your job coach or instructor for feedback.

You can print out the practice objections worksheet on our website.

Objection: _____

Response: _____

Objection: _____

Response: _____

Objection: _____

Response: _____

Make interview practice cards.

Make a set of practice interview cards using 3 × 5 index cards. Use the interview questions worksheet to find questions, or start with some of the questions in this lesson. Write an answer for each question. You can write your answer on the back of the card, but practice answering until you remember the answer without looking at the card. Practice using the dress rehearsal exercise. Have someone ask you questions while you give answers. Be sure to practice responding to, "tell me about yourself."

You can print out the interview questions worksheet on our website.

Make another set of practice cards for objections. Practice your responses to the objections. The more you practice, the better you will do in your interview!

Lesson 6   Taking Care of Details

In life, sometimes the littlest things make the biggest difference. Saying "thank you" or holding a door open can make a good impression. With job interviews, paying attention to little details can sometimes make a big difference.

Imagine that you have practiced and prepared well for an interview, but you get caught in a traffic jam and show up 20 minutes late. What are your chances for the job now? Your practice means nothing, because all the interviewer remembers is that you were late.

Get ready before the day of the interview.

At any job interview, try make a positive first impression. Believe it or not, the first 90 seconds of an interview may determine whether or not you get the job. If you show up one minute late, sweating from running through the parking lot, your first impression will be a bad one. Your odds of success from there will drop. Make sure you plan everything days ahead of time.

1.   **Confirm the address and phone number.**

     Check and double-check the address of your job interview. When you make the appointment, be sure to ask which door to enter, what floor to go to, and which room number you will be in. Make sure you have a phone number to call, just in case.

2.   **Get directions to the building.**

     To make sure you arrive in plenty of time, check online maps or smartphone apps, such as Google Maps or MapQuest, to get directions. Or check the directions on your GPS. Be sure you know exactly where you are going. If it is a place you have not been before, make a trial run the day before to be sure the directions are correct. Allow plenty of time for traffic. Check traffic reports ahead of time. Plan to arrive early, just in case.

3.   **Confirm the time of the interview.**

     Check and double-check the interview time to make sure you know when you need to arrive. Plan enough time for parking, walking from the bus stop, going through security, getting up the elevator or stairs, signing in, or other delays.

     If you think it might take 45 minutes to get there, leave the house 90 minutes early just in case. There may be an accident or construction. You just never know. So give yourself a lot of extra time to get to the interview. If you are taking a train or a bus to your interview, plan to arrive early.

4. **Arrive early to gather your thoughts.**

When you arrive early, you have time to get your résumés, your business cards, your pen, and paper ready. You can relax for a few minutes so you won't seem nervous or rushed. Plan to reach the parking lot at least 30 to 45 minutes early.

Figure out where the closest coffee shop is to the place where you are interviewing. If you arrive very early, you can sit in the coffee shop and review your interview cards. Then you can go to the interview site just 15 minutes early. It is much better to arrive early than late to your job interviews. You'll will feel less stressed and more ready for the interview.

About 15 minutes before your appointment, check the mirror to make sure you are well groomed. Enter the building and check in with the receptionist. Now you have a few minutes to look around and get familiar with the building. You might see some awards or photos on the wall. These could provide some great talking points to use during the interview. You can also get an idea of what the work **environment** is like.

environment – conditions in and around a place

Exercise: My Plan to Arrive for an Interview

Think about one of your target companies. Where is it? Imagine that you have a 9:30 a.m. interview there next Monday morning. Use an online map or your GPS to figure out how to get from your home to the company by 9:15 a.m. For an extra challenge, see if you can find a coffee shop near the interview site. Remember to consider traffic delays, weather, construction, and the time it will take to get from the parking lot to the interview room.

Answer these questions:

1. What time will you need to leave your house? _____

2. Are you driving or taking public transportation? _____

3. If you are driving, where will you park? _____
   (If you need to park in a city garage, allow extra time. Do you need to bring money to pay for parking? Do you need extra time to find a parking space?)

4. If you are taking public transportation, how much time will you need to walk from your stop to the interview site? _____

5. What problems might delay you in getting to the interview site?

   _____

   (traffic accident, construction, bus late, can't find parking space, etc.)

6. Think about your answer to question 1.

   Do you have plenty of time to account for any delays or problems? _____

   Do you need to change the time you leave the house? _____

   If so, what is your new time you plan to leave the house? _____

Arrival timeline

	Leave my house
	Arrive at bus stop or train station
	Get in car/train/bus
	Train/bus leaves
	Arrive at building, parking garage/lot, bus/train stop
	Walk from car/bus/train to building
	Enter building and walk to reception and/or interview room
9:15	Arrive at interview
9:30	Interview begins

Confirm contact information.

pronunciation – the sound of a word

Whenever possible, try to get the exact spelling and **pronunciation** of the interviewer's name. You don't want to make a bad impression by saying the interviewer's name wrong. It shows a lack of respect. If you are not sure, call the company receptionist and ask.

In advance, ask for the names of the interviewers and their contact information. Ask the person who schedules your interview—usually the HR manager or the hiring manager. Ask for each interviewer's name, job title, email address, and phone number. The more you know about your interviewers ahead of time, the greater your chances will be for success. Also, get contact information in case of unplanned problems, such as an accident or car trouble.

The more you know about your interviewers, the more confident you will be. Research the interviewers on the company website or LinkedIn, so that you know who they are and what they do. You will also need this information to follow up with them after the interview. While this may seem to be a small step, it can have a major impact on your success.

Prepare in advance.

Have you ever been in a hurry to get somewhere when you can't find your cellphone or your keys? It seems that the more you rush, the greater the chance that something will go wrong. You don't want to be late to your interview because you can't find something you need or because you discovered at the last minute that your interview clothes are not clean. Don't take the chance that something will go wrong. Going to an interview is stressful enough. Plan ahead to avoid any unpleasant surprises.

Avoid stress by planning ahead.

Set out your interview clothes the day before. Don't risk being late because you cannot find something to wear or because there's something wrong with your clothes. Prepare your interview clothes and accessories the day before your job interview. Decide what you want to wear a few days in advance so that you have time to clean, iron, or mend, if necessary. Make sure your shoes are shined, and your accessories are in good condition. Set out the entire outfit the day before, to be sure everything is ready. How you dress says a lot about you. When you dress professionally, you make a positive first impression.

Set your alarm. Don't take the chance of waking up late on the day of the interview. Even if you are sure you'll be up, set your alarm anyway. Allow plenty of time to wake up, review your practice questions, and get ready for your interview. To be safe, set two alarms, five minutes apart. That way, if the first alarm fails, the second one will wake you up.

Tidy up your car and fill up the gas tank. If you have a car, clean it and fill up the gas tank the day before. If your car is clean, neat, and organized, you will feel less stressed while you drive to the interview. You will be more confident you arrive. Fill the tank the day before so you don't have to worry about it when you leave for the interview.

In some cases, the interviewer may walk you to your car. A clean car will make a good impression. It doesn't matter what kind of car you have, as long as it looks well taken care of and neat. A prospective employer will think that a person who cares about details such as wearing professional clothes and driving a clean car will also care about the details at his or her job.

Pump up your confidence. Listening to music helps some people to relax and get in the proper mood before a job interview. Others might need to exercise or go for a walk. Do whatever works for you. Put yourself in the right frame of mind before the interview. Remind yourself that you are great! Look in your mirror. Pump your fist in the air and yell out, "I am great!"

Most importantly, believe in your ability to succeed. If you have a list of daily affirmations from *WorkWise: Choosing a Job*, repeat them to yourself. If you believe that you are the best candidate for the job, your interviewers will believe it, too!

Define success, expect success, and visualize success.

Before your interview, define your desired outcome. Identify your goal for the interview. Then make a mind picture of that outcome. **Visualize** the interviewer at the end of the interview reaching over the desk, shaking your hand and saying that he or she would like to offer you a job. When you visualize and expect success, you can and will achieve it!

visualize – form a picture in your mind

Follow these last minute tips:

1. Eat lightly before the interview. You don't want to feel hungry, but don't eat anything that will upset your stomach or give you bad breath.

2. Brush your teeth and use mouthwash before the interview. If you have a long **commute**, use a breath mint or spray to freshen your breath just before you walk in. If you chew gum, get rid of it before the interview starts.

3. Turn off your cellphone before you walk in, or leave it in the car. Don't let yourself—or the interviewer—be **distracted** by a buzzing, beeping, or ringing phone.

4. Smile and have fun. Every interview is an exciting learning experience. It could open the door to your new career.

commute – trip to and from a job

distracted – unable to pay attention

You can print out a job interview checklist on our website.

Exercise: Get Ready for My Interview

What do you need to do to be ready for your interview? Check this list. Add anything else you need. Make a plan to get ready for your interview.

I have packed these items in my briefcase or bag:	Yes?
Résumés, business cards, handbills	
References: names and contact information	
All required information for filling out an application	
List of questions for interviewer	
Notepad and pen	
ID or any documentation I need for the job	
Cellphone (turned off during interview)	
I have:	
Confirmed the date, time, and address of the interview	
Interview site: address, directions, and phone number	
Interview clothes: cleaned and pressed	
Cleaned car, filled gas tank, or planned other transportation to interview	
Showered, brushed teeth, combed hair	

Prepare for these four common kinds of interviews:

1. Telephone interviews

2. Face-to-face interviews with one person

3. Face-to-face interviews with a group of people

4. Job fair interviews

Telephone Interviews: Sometimes an employer will ask to interview you by telephone. Likely, this will be a screening interview to help the employer decide who to bring in for a face-to-face interview. You may be asked to do the interview using a video calling app, such as FaceTime or Skype. Employers often find telephone interviews to be a cost-effective and efficient way to narrow the field of applicants during the hiring process. You never know when an employer will call to ask questions. Be ready to speak by phone anytime during business hours. Do you best to find a quiet place to talk if an employer calls you.

When an employer schedules a phone interview, prepare just like you would for a face-to-face interview. Practice your answers to questions and objections. Make sure you have prepared a response to "tell me about yourself." Wear business clothes, so you will feel confident and professional.

Here are some tips for phone interviews:

- Confirm the call time, phone number, and who is planning to make the call.

- Keep your phone line open at least 10 minutes before the call time and at least 15 minutes afterwards. This way, you are sure to get the call, even if the interviewer calls early or late.

- Find a quiet place to have your phone interview. You don't want to be interrupted by television noise or people talking. Focus on the call as if you were in a face-to-face interview.

- If possible, use a landline phone. Cellphones often drop calls. With a landline phone, you may hear each other more clearly. Do not use a speaker phone.

- Remove distractions. A messy room will distract you. If you are on a video interview, the interviewer can see your background. When you have a video interview, turn on the lights and have a bookshelf or plain wall behind you.

- Have a notepad, pen, and calendar ready. If the interview goes well, the interviewer may want to schedule a face-to-face interview.

- Take the interview call standing up or sitting at a desk. If you are on video, sit up straight. Many people find that standing up while talking on a phone interview helps them think and speak more clearly.

- Have your résumé, application, and cover letter in front of you. The interviewer might ask you questions about what you wrote.

- Write out a list of questions to ask and key points to discuss with the employer. Don't rely on your memory.

- During a video interview, keep solid eye contact with the web camera. If you look away too much or don't focus, that will distract the interviewer. Practice with a friend before the interview if you are not used to video calling.

- Make sure you speak clearly so the interviewer can understand you. You may need to speak a little more slowly than usual.

- Smile and have fun. Yes, an interviewer can sense if you are smiling, confident, and having fun on a phone interview. When you smile, your voice will sound better. Be relaxed, but don't overdo it—let the interviewer know that you take this opportunity seriously.

Face-to-Face Interview with One Person: It's very common to have a face-to-face interview with one person. Often an HR Manager will use these interviews to screen candidates. Then a few people will be scheduled for interviews with the hiring manager. This is a chance to show you are the right fit for the position.

Here are some tips for face-to-face interviews:

- Make sure you understand the interviewer's idea of an ideal candidate for the job. Talk about how you fit this idea.

- Try to understand the interviewer's style and personality. Does he or she seem serious or relaxed? Try to match your tone to the interviewer's.

- Ask questions. In the best interviews, the interviewer does most of the talking. Remember to ask about his or her vision of the ideal candidate for the job. Also, ask about the company's expectations for the person they hire for the position.

- Learn about the hiring process. Your goal for the interview is to get to the next step, which could be an offer or a second interview. Ask, "What is the next step in the process?"

- Look for clues that tell you about the interviewer. Does he or she have family pictures on the desk? Are there awards on the wall? Do you see items or photos of items that the company makes? What else do you see?

- Be yourself. Don't try to be someone you are not. Certainly, you want to present your best self. But a good interviewer can tell if you are being fake.

- Be truthful. If you can't get hired by being truthful, then the job is not right for you. Address objections and concerns truthfully and positively.

- Show excitement for the position and confidence that you are the best person for the job.

- Thank the interviewer for his or her time.

- Smile. Try to be as positive as possible throughout the interview. Show how you would be a great addition to the team.

You may have one-on-one interviews with different people in the company. First, treat each person as if he or she is the main decision-maker. You never know whose opinion matters most. Second, get each person's business card. Better yet, find out their names, titles, and contact information ahead of time.

Face-to-Face Interview with a Group: Group interviews are becoming more common. Do not be surprised if you meet two or more people in an interview. Ahead of time, ask the company for the names and titles of the interviewers. Address the interviewers by name.

As always, be prepared. Companies use group interviews when the hiring manager wants different employees to help make the hiring decision.

Treat each person in the group interview as the main decision-maker. Address each person's questions and concerns. Don't forget to get each person's name and contact information so you can properly thank each person after the interview.

Here are some tips for group interviews:

- Greet each person in the room by name: shake hands and introduce yourself. Hand each person your résumé and business card.

- Make eye contact with everyone in the room. A great way to build **rapport** is through eye contact.

  rapport – a friendly relationship (rah POR)

- Keep looking at the friendly faces. Friendly faces are important because they will help build your confidence during the interview.

- Don't look too much at unfriendly faces. In many group interviews, one person may cross arms and frown or look stern. Don't ignore the negative person, but focus more on the positive people.

- Ask open-ended questions like, "Would you describe the ideal candidate for this position, and how that person would work with your team?" This will help you learn what they are really looking for.

- At the end of the interview, ask if there are any more questions or concerns. If so, address them and confirm that they are satisfied with your answers. Then, say to the group, "I am looking forward to working with each of you. I'm excited to become part of your team. What is the next step in this process?" This question shows you are confident and you want the job.

- Shake each person's hand and say thank you.

- Get a complete list of the people you met with. If you did not get their business cards, ask the manager who set up the interview if you could have a list of their names with contact information. You will need the contact information to send each person a thank-you email.

- Send each interviewer a personalized thank-you email within 24 hours of the interview.

Job Fair Interviews: Many candidates attend public job fairs to find job opportunities. Hotels, restaurants, and casinos sometimes hold job fairs to find job candidates. A new shopping center or business complex may hold a job fair for its tenants. During a job fair, a company may receive hundreds of résumés and meet dozens of candidates. A potential employer may ask you a few questions to see if you are a good candidate to interview.

Here are some job fair interview tips:

- Bring your résumés and business cards. If you have a handbills targeted to companies at the fair, bring those as well. Bring a notepad and pen.

- Show each company representative respect. Treat each person at a job fair as a potential employer.

- Dress professionally. Dress as if you were going to an interview. When you meet with a company representative, you may have a screening interview.

- Use your 30-second elevator speech. You won't have a lot of time to talk with people, so you need to quickly make a great impression.

- Smile and be friendly.

- Ask company representatives what they look for in an ideal candidate. Take notes.

- Gather printed items from each company. These brochures and flyers will help you learn more about the company and its jobs.

- Get a business card from each person you meet. Send a personal email to each representative who takes the time to talk to you.

Exercise: What Do I Know about Interviews? What Do I Want to Know?

Review Lessons 4, 5, and 6. Use the K-W-L chart to list five things you now know about job interviews. List five things you want to know. Try to find answers to your questions. Look online or talk to your career counselor or instructor. When you get the answers, fill out the third column of the chart.

K What do I know?	W What do I want to know?	L What have I learned?

As you know, the job interview is the most important activity in the job search process. Regardless of the strength of your résumé, your credentials, or your experience, if you don't perform well in the interview, you won't get the job!

Getting a job interview is like a game show. Thousands of contestants may compete for a chance to appear on a TV game show. They go through several rounds of auditions, interviews, and tests. With each round, people are **eliminated**. Finally, a few people are chosen to appear on the show. And in the end, only one person wins. The job interview process is often very much like that.

eliminated – removed

It's tough to get an interview. Each one is very important. Prepare well and take advantage of every opportunity you get. All this may seem overwhelming, but this workbook can help you to succeed!

You have learned a lot in the last unit about preparing for an interview. In the next unit, you will learn more about the following:

- Preparing for a winning interview (Lesson 7)

- Showing the traits of a good employee (Lesson 8)

- Following up after your interview (Lesson 9)

Self-Check: How Well Do I Show My Value?

When you go on interviews, you need to talk about your key selling points and your value as an employee. How do you show your value? Does the way you look and act match what you say? Before you begin Lesson 7, think about you can show your value by what you wear, how you take care of yourself, and how you act. Imagine you are walking into an interview. List three ways that you can show your value.

_____

_____

_____

_____

_____

While you work through lessons 7, 8, and 9, think about how you show your value and how you can show your value more clearly.

Lesson 7   Preparing for a Winning Interview

Now you know how to prepare for an interview. This lesson focuses on what to do during the interview to ensure that it goes well. You can win at a job interview by using skills that professional salespeople use to win new clients and to sell products or services.

What is a job interview? An interview is a two-way sales call. In one way, you, the candidate, are looking to sell the interviewer on why he or she should hire you. In another way, the interviewer is trying to sell you on why you should work for the company. Remember, interviewing is a two-way street. You may need the job, but the interviewing company needs to fill a position too. Show respect, but also remember that you have something to offer. You have value!

There are five phases to a winning job interview.

Professional salespeople plan before every meeting. At the beginning of a typical sales meeting, salespeople introduce themselves. Next, they establish rapport and build interest. Then they find out what the customer needs. Next, they present their solution or what they are selling. And last, they ask for the order or close the deal.

You can follow the same five-phase approach to have a winning job interview. Your goal is to convince the interviewer that your skills, knowledge, and abilities are worth buying. You are selling yourself.

Phase 1: Greet the interviewer and introduce yourself.

How you introduce yourself is very important. Shake hands, look the interviewer in the eyes, greet him or her, and state your name. It's a good idea to write out a script for how you want to introduce yourself and practice.

Here are some example introductions.

> If you have a job right now, try something like this:
> *"Hi. I'm Bill Lee of XYZ Company. It is a pleasure to meet you."*

> If you are don't have a job, you can say something like this:
> *"Good morning. I'm Bill Lee. It is a pleasure to meet you. I'm excited to have this opportunity to speak to you about working for ABC Corporation."*

The above examples are quick ways to introduce yourself when entering the interview. Practice saying your introduction a few times before the interview. You want to sound relaxed and natural when you greet the interviewer.

After your introductions, wait for the interviewer to sit down. Don't sit down first unless he or she says, "Please be seated." When you sit down first, you show disrespect for the interviewer's **authority**. If you are interviewing with a group, wait for one or two people to sit down before you do.

phases – parts or stages of events

authority – power

Ideally, the next thing to do is to for you and the interviewer to exchange business cards. If you don't have a business card, you may offer the interviewer a copy of your résumé or handbill. If the interviewer does not offer you a card, politely ask for one.

During the first phase your goals are to

- make a positive first impression,

- introduce yourself,

- show respect for the interviewer(s),

- exchange business cards, and

- demonstrate your excitement about the position.

Exercise: My Introduction

Write out your introduction. Practice saying it, until you sound relaxed and natural.

_____

_____

Phase 2: Establish rapport and build interest.

establish – put into place or make happen

The second phase of a successful job interview is to establish rapport with the interviewer and to build some interest. There are several ways you can **establish** rapport. One way is to talk about something you have in common. For example, if you see a picture of a sports team or a team logo, you could say, "Are you a baseball fan too?" The interviewer may say something like, "Did you see last night's game?" Now, you have something you can relate to.

Another way to establish rapport is to ask an open-ended question. Asking, "How long have you been with XYZ Company?" can be a good conversation starter. You can also chat about general topics like sports or weather. Try to keep an upbeat, positive tone. You don't want to start off your interview in a negative way by complaining about the traffic. And don't ask personal questions or bring up controversial topics like religion or politics.

Exercise: My Rapport-Building Questions

To get your interview off to a strong start, you need build rapport. Write down three to five possible questions you can ask to establish rapport. Check with a family member, friend, or instructor for their feedback on your questions. Remember, these questions should make people feel comfortable and want to talk with you.

_____

_____

_____

_____

_____

Phase 3: Review the employer's needs and gather information.

During this phase, find out the expectations and responsibilities of the position to determine if it is the right job for you. You will then know which of your selling points to focus on. You and the interviewer are checking each other out to see if there is a potential fit.

The interviewer will ask you questions. This is where your practice will pay off. Ask open-ended questions to understand what kind of person the employer wants in the job. Here are some questions you can ask to get more information:

- Would you describe your ideal candidate for this job?"
- What are your expectations for the person who fills this position?
- When do you expect to fill the position?

Listen carefully to the answers and take notes. If you need to, ask clarifying questions to be sure you understand the interviewer. A clarifying question asks to make something more clear. For example, "I'm not sure what you meant when you said that the position has flexible hours. Do you mean that I could decide what hours I would like to work?"

Listen twice as much as you talk. Some people say that we have two ears and one mouth for a reason. Good salespeople know they should listen twice as much as they talk when they meet with clients. This is a good rule for most communication. During the job interview, don't think you have to do all the talking. In fact, in the best job interviews, the interviewer talks much more than the candidate does. The more you let the interviewer talk, the more you will find out about the position.

Phase 4: Present your solution—you!

During the fourth phase, you present your solution. The employer needs to fill an open position, and the solution is you. Convince the interviewer why you are the best candidate for the position. During phase 4 of a sales meeting, salespeople present their product or service to the customer. In the job interview, you are presenting and selling yourself. Your goal is to sell or convince the interviewer why he or she should hire you. Share your key selling points that are most important to the interviewer.

Demonstrate to the interviewer that you are the ideal person for the job. Make a closing statement, much like a lawyer in court, to emphasize your best qualities and leave the interviewer with a good impression. First, restate a couple of key points about the position that the interviewer told you. Then, share your key selling points and tell how they will fit the position and benefit the company. Explain why you are the best candidate for this job. Express your confidence that you can do a good job for the company.

Here is an example of a closing statement from Juan Jobseeker for a job with a home health agency:

> *You mentioned that your ideal candidate should be have strong skills as a CNA and truly like working with senior citizens. You also mentioned that one problem you have is that some aides do not complete their records correctly. This job is a great fit for me, because in my last jobs, I sharpened my skills as a CNA in both a hospital setting and in homes. That allows me to provide high quality health care. I have come to enjoy working with seniors in their homes. I also have shown that I have excellent record-keeping skills. With my skills and commitment to the patients, I believe I will be a really strong addition to your team.*

Express the features and benefits of your key selling points. During your interviews, you need to sell interviewers on why they should hire you. Your key selling points may include your skills, knowledge, and personal qualities. Think about which selling points are most important to the interviewer.

Just telling someone you have a certain skill or expertise is not enough. You need to show the interviewer why your key selling points are important. Salespeople talk about "Features, Functions, and Benefits." Your feature is your selling point. The function is the practical application or how you use your key selling point. The benefit is why the selling point matters to the interviewer or the position.

Here are some examples of how to express key selling points as features, functions, and benefits:

> *Feature:* I have five years of experience as a CNA.
> *Function:* With my experience, I have learned a lot about health care and I have developed great skills, especially in working with seniors.
> *Benefit:* This means that I can do effective work for your home health agency right away. You would not need to worry about training me.

> *Feature:* I am a creative person.
> *Function:* I can think of creative ways to solve problems that clients have at mealtimes.
> *Benefit:* This means I can think on my feet when things go wrong. If a client has a problem at a restaurant, I can solve the problem, keep him happy, and ensure that he is willing to come back again.

> *Feature:* I am great at building and making things.
> *Function:* I can do different jobs on a construction site. I am good at more than one job.
> *Benefit:* This means I can work on different jobs at a site. So, if you need drywall installation and framing done, I can do either job well.

Believe in yourself. Believe you are the best candidate for the job, and the interviewer will too! You have to believe you are the best candidate for the job to sell that fact to the interviewers. Interviewers will pick up on your positivity, and they will think positively about you.

Exercise: Feature, Function, and Benefits of My Key Selling Points.

Think about your key selling points. Explain the Feature, Function, and Benefit of three key selling points.

Feature: _____

Function: _____

Benefit: _____

Feature: _____

Function: _____

Benefit: _____

Feature: _____

Function: _____

Benefit: _____

Phase 5: Overcome objections and go for the close.

In the final phase, you should go for the close, or ask for what you want. At a job interview, you will ask to move to the next step in the decision-making process.

There is a right way and a wrong way to do this. The wrong way is to ask, "When should I expect to hear back from you?" or "Do you have any final concerns?" These questions do not make you sound confident. They can make the interviewer feel uncomfortable.

Here is an example of the right way to close the deal:

> *I am very excited about this opportunity. There seems to be a good match between the company's needs and what I can offer. What is the next step in this process?*

Now, that is a strong close. You are showing excitement. You are showing confidence. You also show that you want the job. And you are asking to move the process forward. The more confident you are, the more confident the interviewer will be in your ability to succeed.

Here is another example of how to close the deal:

> *I want this job. From what you have told me, this seems to be a perfect fit. What is the next step in the hiring process?*

Overcome objections and close again. When you make your closing, you may find out that the interviewer has some objections. This is your chance to respond to them.

Objections are possible concerns that the interviewer might have about you. Sometimes an objection is real and clear, and other times the interviewer may not describe the objection. Remember, an objection can actually mean the interviewer is interested in hiring you and just wants to be sure he or she is making the right decision.

If you give your closing statement and ask about the next step, but you don't get the reaction you hoped for, the interviewer may have an objection. Look at this example:

> *You:* "What is the next step in the hiring process?"
> *Interviewer:* "I need to show your résumé to some other people to get their feedback."

At this point, you can't tell if this is real objection, or if the interviewer is stalling or making excuses. Try to get more information, while sounding positive and confident:

> *You:* "I can appreciate that. If everyone else likes my résumé, is there anything that would keep you from hiring me?"

This is a direct question to find out if the interview has an objection:

> *Interviewer:* "Well not exactly. I am concerned about the fact that you have had three jobs in the last four years."

Now you have found the real objection, you need to quickly think of a way to respond:

> *You:* "I can understand where you are coming from. If I were in your position, I would likely have the same concern. While I had planned to stay with each job for a long time, it just didn't work out that way. During the recession, I was laid off because I was the newest employee. You don't want to have to hire a new person after only a year, and I sure don't want have to look for a new job after a year. This position is a great fit with my skills and experience, and I know I will be an excellent long-term employee. Do you have any other questions about how I can be a good fit for your team?"
> Interviewer: "No, I think you addressed my concerns."

Okay great! You have addressed the interviewer's concerns. Now, confirm that's true and see if the interviewer is willing to discuss next steps:

> *You:* "Great! I am really excited about this position. What is the next step in the process?"

Hopefully, by now, the interviewer is willing to explain what happens next. You should be able to tell if the interviewer seems excited about you becoming part of the team and if he or she wants to speak with you again. If you still get a lukewarm response, you may need to ask again if there are any other concerns:

> *You:* "I still sense you have some concerns. Is there anything else that would keep you from recommending me for this job?"

Either the interviewer will answer your question or he or she will simply say no. At this point, you have done all you can do.

So, now, show the proper respect and gratitude, even if it seems like you are not getting the job. If the interviewer says, "Look, I just don't think you are the right fit," then be gracious. Express your appreciation for being considered.

gratitude – a feeling of thankfulness

gracious – polite and friendly

Here is an example of a gracious response:

> I understand. I greatly appreciate you taking time to meet with me today. If, in the future, your needs change, I hope you will keep me in mind. Once again, thank you so much for the opportunity.

Be respectful and don't burn any bridges by being negative. You may get an opportunity to apply to the same company for a different position. If you don't get this job, focus on the positives. You made some contacts at a great company and learned more about a job that you are interested in. Use this experience to improve your chances when you apply for the next job.

On the other hand, you may leave with the feeling that the company is ready to make you an offer. Don't be overconfident, but leave your interview on a positive note. Here are some suggested closing comments, if it looks like you are going to get the job:

> Great. I can't thank you enough for the opportunity. I can't wait to start.

> I am very excited about this opportunity. I look forward to touching base early next week. Once again, thank you so much.

> I am thrilled about this opportunity. I look forward to talking more and I really think that I can be a strong member of your team. Thank you so much for taking time to meet with me today.

These responses are more powerful and positive than just saying, "Thanks for your time. I look forward to hearing from you."

Exercise: My Gracious Responses

Write two gracious responses. Write one for an interview that has gone well. Write another for a situation where it looks like you will not get the job.

_____

_____

_____

_____

_____

_____

Always be gracious and honest.

Part of being gracious is never saying anything bad about a past employer. If you were laid off or fired from a job, you may feel angry. But interviewers don't want to hear about it. Employers look for people who can get along with a team. If you complain about your past boss, the interviewer will likely think that you do not get along well with others. Employers will wonder if you would talk negatively about them.

An interviewer may ask you why you were let go from your last job. You want to respond truthfully, but focus on your positive qualities. Here are some example answers:

> *While my boss was a great manager with a solid track record, his (or her) management style did not allow me to perform at my best.*

> *I greatly enjoyed the job and my boss. However, due to the poor economy the company had to lay off people. Because I was a new employee, I was one of the first to be laid off.*

Never make negative comments about a job or a boss, like these:

- I hated my last boss.

- My boss had no clue.

- The company was terrible.

- I worked with a bunch of losers.

- I couldn't wait to get out of that company.

Interviewers will not recommend you for the job if you speak badly about past employers.

Don't lie about anything in an interview. Lying about your skills and qualifications will not help you. When you lie, your body language and your eyes will usually give you away. And you probably will not get the job. Companies have ways of checking your credentials. If you do get the job after lying on your résumé, or during the interview, you may be terminated later. Most companies have policies that say that lying on a résumé or in the interview process is grounds for termination.

When you tell the truth, you don't have to remember what you said.
—Margot Bermont

Lesson 8   Practicing Traits of Good Employees

Did you know that more than 90 percent of all communication in any conversation is nonverbal? That means that you need to pay attention not only to what you say in an interview, but also to what you don't say. Employers do not just rely on résumés and applications to decide which people to hire. Employers use interviews to learn more about a candidate's skills and to see if the candidate has the right traits to be successful on the job. They will look for nonverbal clues that you have important **traits**.

traits – qualities or noticeable features

Here are some traits interviewers look for in a new employee.

1.   They have a similar personality.

Think about the type of people who are your best friends. Do they have interests, motivations, and values similar to yours? If you are like most people, your closest friends will have similar personalities to yours. Most hiring managers tend to hire employees who mirror their personalities and drive, in one respect or another. This is why you should build rapport during the interview by talking about something you have in common.

2.   They are low maintenance, self-driven, and trustworthy.

Most managers hate dealing with problem employees because that leaves less time for them to get work done. So employers want to hire people who will not need lots of extra attention. Hiring managers look for **low-maintenance**, **motivated**, trustworthy people. Trust is one of the most important parts of a successful manager and employee relationship.

low-maintenance – not needing a lot of attention
motivated – excited or eager

Managers usually don't mind helping employees improve their skills or solve real problems. For the most part, managers want to help their employees grow and succeed. However, managers do not like employees they can't trust or who don't have the drive and motivation to work hard and do a good job. Managers don't want to deal with small problems. Managers don't like wasting time on team members who don't get along. Managers also don't like it when employees miss work without a **valid** reason. Perhaps worst of all, managers lose sleep when they no longer trust an employee.

valid – acceptable or reasonable

Managers don't mind when mistakes are made because an employee is trying. What managers do mind are mistakes made because of lack of effort or not paying attention. The best relationship between an employee and a manager is when they trust each other and when both try to do the best they can. That is why hiring managers don't want to hear a lot of negativity during the interview. They are looking for signs that you can be trusted.

3. They have a positive attitude toward the job and co-workers.

If you come to the interview with a frown on your face and in a bad mood, few people will want to hire you. You need to show that you have a positive attitude about the job and your potential co-workers.

Managers hate when one employee fights with another employee over unimportant matters. The last thing a manager needs is conflict among team members. Therefore, when the employer interviews a candidate, he or she wants to see how well that person will get along with the rest of the team and with the company as a whole. So, the employer will watch how you treat each person you meet and how you act to see if you are a match.

4. They are goal-oriented and efficient.

goal-oriented – working hard to achieve plans or goals

Goal-oriented individuals tend to be more productive and efficient than those who are not. Employers are not just looking for hard workers, but they look for employees who are smart workers. They want people who make good use of their time and effort.

Do you start the week with a To-Do list? People who make a To-Do list and stick to it are usually more effective and get more accomplished. Goal-oriented people get things done.

5. They are problem-solvers, not problem-creators.

Managers hate having employees who cause more problems than they solve. Therefore, hiring managers will reject any potential candidate who might create problems.

Managers don't mind dealing with real problems. In fact, how well an employee helps to solve a problem can really show his or her value to the organization. Most managers want their employees to come up with possible solutions so they can discuss them. Then the managers can decide on the best solution.

Managers really do not want problems that could be avoided. Problems that really upset managers include personality conflicts among employees, rude or illegal communication between employees, and problems caused by employees not doing their jobs.

6. They are competent.

competent – able to do a job well

Next, the interviewer will look for somebody who is **competent**, and can do the job well. Nobody wants to hire someone who may do a bad job. Instead, hiring managers want to know that the candidate can either do the job well now or show that he or she can learn the job fast.

Exercise: How Can I Show My Best Traits?

Remember that words are important, but they are not enough to show your best traits. Think about which of the listed traits you have. Using the chart below, list the trait and a verbal way that you could express the trait to an interviewer. Then list a nonverbal way that you could show the trait to an interviewer or hiring manager. Read the sample first.

Trait	Verbal expression	Nonverbal expression
I am trustworthy.	My work attendance record shows that I had only two sick days last year, and that I was on time every day.	I will show up on time to the interview with all my required paperwork.

About 90 percent of communication is nonverbal.

In an interview, verbal communications, or the words you use, will tell the interviewer whether you are qualified for the job. However, your nonverbal communication will bring about negative or positive emotions for the interviewer.

nonverbal – not spoken or stated

Hiring managers tend to hire employees who are similar to themselves, often without realizing it. Interviewers feel more comfortable with people who seem like them not only in mindset but also in nonverbal ways. Fair or not, employers often respond positively or negatively to how people look, sound, feel, and smell. So, pay attention to what you communicate nonverbally.

Pay attention to your look.

When you arrive for the interview, your appearance sends a message about how seriously you take the job interview and how much you really want the job. A professional appearance communicates confidence and seriousness about the work. Several factors contribute to your overall appearance.

Clothing. When you show up for the interview, whether in person or over the phone, are you dressed professionally? Believe it or not, even over the phone, interviewers can sense how you are dressed. For your next phone interview, wear clothes you would wear to work or to an interview, and see how much better you do.

going overboard – doing too much or going too far

business casual – a way of dressing for work that is less formal than business suits

It used to be easy to know what to wear on an interview. Most everyone wore business suits. Now, that is not the case. So, what should you wear? Wear the most professional attire possible without going overboard. The best guide is to dress like the most successful people who have that job. In other words, find out what most people wear and dress just a little nicer.

For many job interviews, business casual is acceptable. For example, if you interview for a job in construction or at a restaurant, wear a business casual outfit. This means clean, pressed slacks or a skirt with a dress shirt or blouse. However, if you are interviewing for a manager job, you should dress the part. Wear a suit and tie or a professional-looking skirt suit or dress.

Here are two ways to find out what you should wear for an interview:

1. If you know someone at the company, ask what people in your type of job wear each day. If they wear casual clothes or a uniform, wear business casual clothes to the interview. If they wear business casual clothes every day, you should probably wear a suit.

2. Search online for "What should I wear to an interview for a _____ job?" You will likely get a number of good answers.

When in doubt, dress a little more formally than you think you should. When wearing a suit, you can always remove a jacket, but you cannot make jeans look more formal. If you are interviewing for a manager position, wear a business suit.

Make sure you understand what business casual clothing is. Here are some general rules:

*   No jeans. Wear nice dress pants in a solid color: gray, navy blue, or black. Pants should fit well and not be baggy or show underwear.

*   No short skirts. Skirts or dresses should fall no shorter than one inch above the knee.

*   No T-shirts. Wear a dress shirt with a collar. The best colors are white, light blue, or light gray.

*   No low-cut tops. Button your blouse or wear a top that doesn't reveal too much skin.

*   No flip-flops, sandals, or sneakers. Wear dress shoes that do not show your toes.

*   Not too much color. Use bright colors carefully, in scarves or ties. You can use red, blue, and green, but don't use the brightest shades.

Preparing your interview clothes can be tricky. Don't be afraid to ask a professional you respect for advice on your interview clothes. You can also check in your area for workforce organizations or places that can provide guidance and clothing. Dress for Success helps women: www.dressforsuccess.org. Career Gear helps men: www.careergear.org.

You can find help with interview clothing at these websites.

The clothes you wear are certainly important, but you should also pay attention to their condition. If you wear a stained and wrinkled suit or a dress that is too tight, you will not make a good impression. Make sure your clothes are cleaned and ironed. Try them on beforehand to make sure they fit well and look good. For best results, clean and iron your clothes two days before the interview, so you won't have to worry at the last minute. If your clothes need dry cleaning, take them to the cleaners a week ahead of time.

Exercise: Inventory Your Professional Clothes

Check your professional clothes. Are they in good shape? Do they have stains or tears? Do you need a new business suit or business casual clothes? Make a short list here of clothes you have and clothes you may need.

_____

_____

_____

_____

_____

Clothes I have	**Clothes I need**
_____	_____
_____	_____
_____	_____
_____	_____

Jewelry and tattoos. Your jewelry says a lot about you. Unless you are interviewing for a very creative position, such as an artist, avoid wearing a lot of jewelry. Choose one or two tailored pieces, like a watch and simple earrings. Wearing a wristwatch shows that you manage your time. Don't wear the following to an interview:

- Big or long dangling earrings
- More than two earrings in each ear
- Studs or rings on the face, lip, eyebrows, or nose
- Ankle bracelets and toe rings
- More than two rings on each hand

Tattoos are not popular with most employers. Some companies have more relaxed policies, once you get the job. It's best to be conservative at the interview and cover up your tattoos, if possible. Wear clothing that covers them. You don't want the interviewer to focus on your tattoos instead of your qualifications.

Grooming. Your hairstyle also tells a lot about you. If your hair is freshly cut and nicely groomed, that gives the impression that you take care of yourself. If your hair is messy or dirty, you can give the opposite impression. If you can, treat yourself to a professional haircut a few days before the interview. If you color your own hair, choose a natural color and do a touch-up before the interview so your roots don't show.

You may not pay much attention to how you dress and groom every day, but an interview is a special occasion. The first impression you give an interviewer is what you look like. You want your appearance to show that you are professional, smart, and capable. Dress like you are a valuable employee who deserves the job!

Here are some other factors to consider about your appearance:

posture – the position of your body

Posture is another form of nonverbal communication. Some interviewers may sit casually, slouch, or cross their legs. Other interviewers will sit straight at a desk. Follow the lead of the interviewer. If has very straight posture, then sit up straight. This way you show through nonverbal communication that you are like the interviewer.

Facial expressions communicate more than words. If the interviewer has a very serious facial expression, you should look serious too. Take your cues from the interviewer. If instead, the interviewer is smiling and friendly, then relax and smile.

Eye contact is very important. Try to look your interviewer in the eyes. When you look directly into the interviewer's eyes, you show that you are confident and that you believe in what you say. In the U.S., looking people in the eye shows that you are honest and trustworthy. It's also a sign of respect to look at the interviewer when he or she is speaking to you. It shows that you are paying attention. Don't look around the room while the interviewer is talking. That makes you look like you don't care or you are not listening.

In some countries, it's disrespectful to look people directly in the eye. But, in the U.S., bosses expect their workers to look at them. They may not trust an employee who does not. If you are not used to looking at someone's eyes when you speak, practice this with friends, family, or classmates.

Pay attention to how you sound.

Your voice matters. Use these tips to speak properly in an interview.

volume – the loudness of a sound

Volume. Have you ever heard someone say, "Use your inside voice?" Teachers often tell children to use their inside voices, to teach them to lower the volume. In general, if you are inside, for example, in an office, you don't need to speak loudly for another person to hear you. In some situations, we need to speak more loudly, so people can hear us. If you are interviewing in an office, speak clearly and do not yell.

You will meet some interviewers who talk loudly and others who speak softly. The best advice is to take your cues from the interviewer. When you interview with a person who talks louder and faster, try to match his or her volume and pace. When you interview with someone who talks softer and slower, then you can slow down and speak more softly.

Tone of voice. Tone is not what you say but the way you say it. You can say something right but use a nasty tone. Tone of voice can be positive or negative, upbeat or depressing, angry or cheerful. Try to speak with a kind, positive tone. One way to do this is to smile. If you smile during the interview, your tone will match your expression.

Pay attention to the way you touch an interviewer.

The only time you touch an interviewer is probably when you shake hands. If you shake hands when you first meet and again as you are leaving, your first and last impressions are your touch. The quality of your handshake can send a strong message about you. If your hands are sweaty or clammy, people may see you as nervous and not confident. However, if your hands are dry and you shake firmly, you send a message that you are confident and capable.

It's normal to be nervous at an interview and when meeting someone new. If you feel your hands getting sweaty, go to the restroom right before your interview and wash your hands with lots of soap and warm water. The soap will dry your hands out, and the warm water will make your hands feel warmer when you shake hands. Then, dry your hands completely. If you can't get to the restroom, bring a handkerchief or tissue in your pocket or purse. Wipe your hands on it before you go into the interview room.

The best possible handshake is firm enough to show confidence, but not so hard that you hurt the person's hand. Squeeze the other person's hand gently. A weak handshake, when you hold the person's hand too loosely, can send a message that you are not confident or that you are not honest. Practice your handshake as often as you can with your job coaches, instructors, and other students. Ask for feedback to make sure get it right.

Pay attention to the way you smell.

Smell is very powerful. What do you feel when you smell your favorite food? How do you feel when you smell something terrible? People react strongly to both good and bad smells. People often react negatively to the scent of someone who does not wear deodorant. Most U.S. businesses expect their employees to shower each day, wear deodorant, and smell clean. Also, wash your work clothes regularly so they do not smell of body odor, food, or cigarette smoke. If an interviewer smells your body odor or dirty clothes, he or she is likely to have a negative reaction to you.

offensive – unpleasant

At the same time, don't use too much cologne or perfume. Avoid wearing any strong scents. Many people are allergic to perfume, or they find strong scents offensive. You don't want to set off someone's allergies during an interview. So, it is best to be freshly showered and wear deodorant, so you smell clean when you go for an interview. If you use perfume or cologne, use very little.

Also, bad breath does not make a good impression. If you smoke, try to avoid smoking right before your interviews, as some hiring managers will not like the smell. Whether or not you smoke, if possible, use breath spray or brush your teeth right before the interview so your breath smells clean.

If you smoke, don't smoke in your car right before the interview. If you do, the smoke will get into your clothes and you will smell strongly of cigarette smoke. That is not the first impression you want to make. Pay attention to these little details in order to make the best impression at an interview.

Exercise: My Nonverbal Communication

Think about all the ways you communicate without speaking. Consider how you look, sound, touch, and smell. Fill out the chart with your plan for how you will manage these details for every interview.

Look	Sound
_____	_____
_____	_____
_____	_____

My Nonverbal Communication

Touch	Smell
_____	_____
_____	_____
_____	_____

Lesson 9　Following Up After the Interview

In *WorkWise: Choosing a Job*, you worked hard to gain confidence, define the job you want, and write your cover letter and résumé. In this book, you networked to find a job opening and practiced and prepared for your interview. Did you follow all the suggestions in this workbook? Are you ready for an interview? If so, what about after the interview? It's just as important to follow up afterward as it is to prepare beforehand.

To make sure your hard work pays off, learn about these three follow-up activities:

1.　Learning from your interview
2.　Thanking people
3.　Checking in with the employer

Proper follow-up will reinforce the good impression you made.

The only way to achieve a positive outcome is to follow up after the interview. During an interview, you might forget to get a business card from the interviewer. Or, the interviewer may not have a business card to give you. You may forget the answer to a question and tell the interviewer that you'll get back to him or her later. If you forgot to state a key selling point during the interview, you can include it in your follow-up email or thank-you note.

Learn from your job interview.

This first step is for your benefit. As soon as you can after the interview, write down your thoughts. List what went well first. Then list any mistakes or things you might have said or handled better. Don't worry about the mistakes you made, but try to learn from them. As you go to more interviews, you will get better at the process. Your confidence will grow.

If you interviewed with more than one person, make notes about each person, especially what he or she said was important for the job. If the interviewer commented on a specific skill you have that is right for the job, make a note. This gives you specific points to mention in your thank-you note.

No interview is bad, as long as you learn from it.

Each interview gives you a chance to learn something that can make you a better candidate in the future. No job interview is a failure if you learn something from it. You may learn how to better describe your key selling points, you may learn how to be less nervous, you may even make a mistake and learn about something you should not do.

After the interview, follow these four steps.

1. **List the main points discussed during the interview.** Right away after your interview, write down the main discussion points while they are fresh in your mind. Find a quiet place like a local coffee shop, library, or bookstore—or even your car—where you can write your notes.

   Writing notes for yourself will help you decide what to write in your thank-you notes. When writing thank-you notes, you can include selling points you did not get to share during the interview. If you remember a question you couldn't answer, you could address that in your thank-you note.

   Here is an example of how you could highlight a key point from the interview:

   During our conversation, you mentioned that one of the greatest challenges you have is finishing projects on time. In my last job, I helped Build-It Construction meet 95 percent of their deadlines on time or early. I look forward to helping your team achieve the same kind of results.

2. **Note any questions or concerns you might have.** After the interview, are you still as excited about the job as you were before the interview? Do you still feel good about the company or the hiring manager? Ask yourself these questions. While you may need a job, if you are feeling less excited or more worried, that could be a warning that the job is not a good fit. Time is valuable, especially during the job search. Stay focused on the positions that make the most sense for you.

   Key questions to ask yourself after an interview include:

   * Would I work well with this boss?
   * Is the job what I thought it was?
   * Would I like working there?
   * Is there a positive attitude around the company?
   * Do the employees seem motivated and happy to be there?
   * Do I have any questions or concerns that were not answered well?

   How much do you want the job? Your answers to these questions will help you decide how to follow up. If you are still excited about the position, then try to make the most impact with your follow-up. Even if you are not excited, be polite and gracious, and write thank-you emails to the interviewers. If you decide to reject the opportunity, tell the interviewer politely that you are withdrawing your application. Thank the company for their time. Always be professional, be polite, and don't burn any bridges.

3. **Note any key selling points you forgot to mention in the interview.** During job interviews, sometimes you forget to share a key selling point. Or the interviewer moves the conversation along so quickly that you don't get a chance to discuss an important qualification. Maybe, after the interview, you realize you totally forgot to mention a very important experience. Don't get mad at yourself about forgetting something. Often, you can make the point in your thank-you

note. One reason to review the interview right away is to note anything you would still like to share with the employer.

Ask yourself questions like these:

- Was there anything important I forgot to say?
- Is there a key selling point I wished I had stated?

List items you forgot to mention. Then, when you are writing your thank-you notes, include those points. Remember these points as you practice for your next interview.

4. **Rate your performance on the job interview, and identify areas to improve.** Reflect on how well you did, so you can do better the next time. Like most things, good interviews take lots of practice. You will make mistakes, but you are a winner if you learn from your mistakes. And, you are a winner just for going to the interview! When you review your interview performance, focus on three key areas: your strengths, your weaknesses, your learning experiences.

Your strengths—When rating your performance, first list what you did well on the interview. Did you introduce yourself well? Did the interviewer seem interested in your key selling points? Did you ask good open-ended questions? Write down all of the things you did right. One way to improve your interviewing skills is to keep doing what works well, and to improve on what did not go well.

Your weaknesses—Now note those areas where you did not do as well. Maybe you feel like you talked too much. Maybe you had a weak answer to a question. Maybe you forgot the answer to a question. Write down whatever you could have improved. As long as you know what to focus on, you can improve these skills.

After an interview, most candidates will think, "I wish I had done something differently." Nobody is perfect. And we all want to do better. Identify the areas where you think you could have done better, so you can learn. Often, you will find simple ways to practice and improve.

Your learning experiences—Don't think of a bad interview as a failure. Look at the things you did well as your strengths. And think of the things you could do better as opportunities to learn.

Not everything that goes wrong at an interview can be fixed. The interview may take a bad turn because of something the interviewer says or does. Identify some things that you believe you could improve. Perhaps you didn't have a good response to an objection. Maybe you weren't fully prepared, so you didn't have the answer to an important question. Whatever it is, write down an improvement plan. Be specific about what you can do to improve:

- I need to practice responding to objections.
- I need to spend more time practicing my introduction.
- I need to ask my teacher for help making eye contact when I speak.

You can print out the job interview review worksheet on our website. Use it to learn from every interview.

When you learn from an interview, no matter the outcome, you benefit from the experience. You should gain something from every interview. Every no brings you one step closer to a yes. The more you can learn from an interview, the greater your chances of doing well at your next interview.

Rate yourself on each phase of the job interview by asking yourself these questions:

- Greeting and introduction: How well did your introduction go?
- Building rapport and generating interest: Did you get along well with the interviewer? Did you feel the interviewer was interested in what you had to say?
- Reviewing needs and gathering information: Did you ask open-ended questions? Did you get enough information about the job?
- Presenting your solution: Did you share your key selling points to convince the interviewer you are right for the job?
- Overcoming objections and closing: Did you overcome any objections? Did you end the interview on a positive note?

Exercise: My Interview Strengths and Weaknesses

Even if you have not had an interview yet, you may have some ideas of your strengths and weaknesses. Fill out this chart. Then complete the sentence to make a plan to build up your strengths and address your weaknesses.

Interview Strengths	Interview Weakness

To build up my strengths, I will _____

To work on my weaknesses, I will _____

Sending a thank-you note is an important part of follow-up.

Why is thanking people important? One reason is to be polite by thanking interviewers for taking the time to speak to you. Another reason is that it is one more chance to make a positive impression.

First, decide which people you should thank. When you interview with just one person, send that person a thank-you email or card. However, you may want to think about other people. If you apply to a position at a large company, you may speak with someone in HR who gave you contact names or information about openings. Or, maybe you met with someone at a job fair, who recommended that you speak to a hiring manager about an interview. When possible, send each person who helped set up the interview a thank-you email. If someone helped you to get the interview, send that person a thank you too. If an administrative assistant or HR manager scheduled the interview, send that him or her a thank-you email.

Treat everyone like a decision-maker.

You never know who can impact the final hiring decision. When you go to an interview, make sure you get business cards from each person you meet. If for some reason, you didn't get a business card, call the company and ask for the contact information.

Who should I follow up with after an interview?

- An HR manager or job fair representative who referred you
- An administrative assistant who gave you information or helped set up a meeting
- The interviewer
- A networking contact who referred you to the company or to the hiring manager

Send a thank-you note to every person who helps you during the interview process.

Should I send an email or a handwritten note?

These days, it's very common for job seekers to send thank-you notes by email. In most cases, a thank-you email is a good choice. People will receive your note right after the interview. But if you really want to make a good impression, mail a handwritten card to the interviewer and/or hiring manager. Make sure your handwriting is neat, and check your writing for errors. Choose a simple, blank notecard or a card that just says, "thank you." Mail the card promptly after the interview.

Send any requested information.

The hiring manager may ask you to provide additional information. Perhaps he or she wants a list of references or a transcript that shows that shows your course grades or a certification. Gather any requested information immediately after the interview. Email it and ask for confirmation of receipt or drop it off personally, so you are sure the information has been received.

Remember these five goals of proper follow-up:

1. Say thank you. Thank interviewers for their time and interest.
2. Show enthusiasm for the job.
3. Restate your key selling points.
4. Share any important information you did not get to in the interview.
5. Express your desire to be part of the team.

Thank each person separately.

After each interview, send a separate and personal thank-you email to each person you met. Just sending one email at once to everyone with your thanks does not show personal attention and probably make people feel less valued.

At a minimum, send an email directly to each person's company email address. If you don't have the email addresses, call the company or check the company website. If you can't get a person's email address, then send a handwritten thank-you note by mail to the company address.

Send thank-you notes right away.

Ideally, you should send a thank-you email on the same day you interview, or within 24 hours of your interview. The best time to send a thank-you email is when you return home after the interview. Review your notes from the interview, and think about how it went. If you take a little time to reflect, you will know if there is something important you need to add to your thank-you note. Quick follow-up shows that you really want the job.

If you don't have your own computer, go to a nearby library or job center to send thank-you emails. Do not wait more than 24 hours after the interview to say thank you.

Why is follow-up important?

Why should you work this hard on follow-up? It is simple. It shows how serious you are about the job. Even more importantly, follow-up often gives you a chance to remind the hiring manager why he or she should hire you.

Sometimes interviewers will interview several candidates in a day or a week. A good thank-you email will help you stand out from the rest of the candidates. In your email, you can also address a concern or objection that came up during the interview, in case you did not have a good answer at the time. Also, when you send a thank-you email, you can mention a key point that you might have forgotten to make during the interview.

It pays to be gracious. Even if you are no longer interested in the position after the interview, send a quick note of thanks. If you send a thank-you email and politely say you are no longer pursuing the job, people will respect your honesty. You never know when you may meet that manager or apply at that company again. Don't burn any bridges.

For a job opportunity you feel strongly about, consider sending both a thank-you email and a handwritten note to the interviewer and/or the hiring manager. Sometimes receiving a handwritten note in the mail can make a real difference to an interviewer. It might be the one extra step that other candidates did not bother to take.

Here is a sample thank-you email:

To: HiringManager@HC Health Care

Subject: Thank you for the interview today

Dear Dr. Employer:

> If the person gave permission, you can use a first name, otherwise be formal.

Thank you for taking time to meet with me today to talk about the home health aide job. In the interview, you mentioned that it was important to have reliable aides. I wanted you to know that my attendance record at my last job was excellent. I always arrive at my clients' homes at least 10 minutes before my shift. Also, my supervisor praised me for doing my paperwork correctly and on time.

> Express thanks and include a key selling point that was missed during the interview.

During our meeting, you also said you were concerned that I would want to work at a hospital. I want you to know that I have worked both in a hospital and in home health care. From that experience, I found that I really enjoy the one-on-one attention I can give clients in their homes. I like to spend time with senior citizens. I always learn so much from them.

> Respond to an objection or concern that came up in the interview.

I look forward to the next step and to becoming part of your team.

> Express excitement and confidence about the job.

Sincerely,

> Use professional closing.

Juan Jobseeker

> Use both first and last name.

Exercise: My Thank-You Note

To make it easy to send a thank-you email quickly, write a sample note. Read the model thank-you note, above. Write your own model note, using your own words. Change the note each time to tailor it to the person, job, and situation.

Dear _____

_____

_____

_____

_____

_____

Sincerely,

_____

Check in with the employer.

After sending your email, what you do next? When you left the interview, did you remember to ask how long it would be before you hear from the company? If not, call the HR manager after the interview and ask.

Perhaps the interviewer said he or she would contact you in a week or two. Maybe no time commitment was made. Maybe the interviewer told you that you should hear something within a week, but you don't. After a week or so, it's okay to call and ask where things stand. When you call, if you get the interviewer's voicemail, leave an upbeat, short message. Consider something like this:

> *Hi, Dr. Employer, this is Juan Jobseeker. I spoke with you last week about the home health aide position. I just wanted to touch base to thank you again for your time and consideration. I was hoping to get an update on your decision-making process. This is an exciting opportunity, and I look forward to hearing from you.*
>
> *I can be reached by email at juan.jobseeker@email.com or by phone at 555-123-4567. Thanks so much, and have a great day.*

If you do reach the person on the phone, keep the call brief. The interviewer or manager is a busy person. Consider saying something like this:

> *Hi, Dr. Employer, this is Juan Jobseeker. I know your time is valuable, so I'll be brief. First, thank you again for meeting with me last week to discuss the home health aide position. I am really impressed with your company and your team. I was wondering if you had an update on where things stand with the open position?*

Don't make interviewers feel uncomfortable. Don't ask if they are going to hire you. Don't put the interviewer on the spot. Just ask politely for the status of the hiring process.

Use a phrase like one of these:

- I just wanted to touch base to see where things stand with the position.
- I am really interested in the position, and I was wondering if you had an update on the decision-making process?

By asking about the hiring process, you won't put the interviewer on the spot. If the interviewer is vague or says, "I don't know," then ask a follow-up question, such as this: "I am very interested in the position. Could you recommend next steps I should take?"

When you speak with the interviewer on the phone, be polite, show enthusiasm, and get an idea where you stand.

What if you don't get the job?

If you do not get a job offer, consider following up with the interviewer to get more information. Here are some reasons to follow up:

- To learn how to improve for future interviews
- To keep your name in the interviewer's mind for future opportunities
- To get a referral for another opportunity
- If the first-choice candidate refuses the offer, you could still get an offer
- Another position may open

Follow up after a bad interview or a rejection.

Following up after a rejection is tough to do, but it's worth the effort. You can learn a lot from an interview that went badly or a position that you lose out on. It is difficult to make a follow-up call after a bad experience, so most people avoid it. However, rejection is a part of the job-search process. You can't take rejection personally. It is a part of interviewing.

Each rejection gets you that much closer to your ideal job. Everything happens for a reason. If you were rejected for the position, it was not the right job for you.

Here is an example of how to follow up after a rejection:

You: Hi, Mr. Stevens. I got your message saying that I did not get the position. I am disappointed, because it was a great opportunity. However, I respect your decision. Just for my information, I was wondering if you could tell me why I wasn't chosen. I'd like to be more prepared for the next time.

Interviewer: You were a good candidate. Unfortunately, another candidate came in who had more experience.

You: I can respect that. I appreciate your honesty. Before I go, I was wondering if you had any suggestions for other employers I could contact.

Interviewer: Well, actually, I think STAR Company is looking for someone like you. You might want to contact Larry Jackson. I'll give you his number.

You: Thank you so much. If for some reason things don't work out with the candidate you selected, I would welcome the opportunity to talk again. I think you have a great company. Thank you so much for your time, and thank you for the referral.

Make your rejection follow-up by phone. Don't send an email. Interviewers are less likely to respond or to explain why you were rejected, if you email. They may also hesitate to give you a referral idea in writing. When you call, it's more personal. An interviewer may respect you for being able to call and ask for advice after a rejection.

Now that you have finished this workbook, you are more likely to have winning interviews. Getting a job is hard work, but you can do it! Review what you have learned in this workbook and keep up your efforts. You are a winner and you will succeed!

ITEM #2191

WorkWise

Getting a Job

WorkWise is a series to help students and job seekers find, get, and keep a job. Three books cover the soft skills that students need for the job search, interview process, and to succeed in the workplace.

Getting a Job

✓ Conducting the Job Search

✓ Preparing for Interviews

✓ Interviewing to Win

In *WorkWise: Getting a Job*, students learn about the hiring process and the best ways to search for a job. Then they prepare for the interview and practice answering interview questions. Finally, they learn the importance of following up after an interview and how they can learn from each interview.

Also available:

WorkWise: Choosing a Job and WorkWise: Starting a Job

Includes FREE online resources:

- Printable worksheets
- Links to career resources
- Practice interview questions
- Job interview checklist

ProLiteracy
New Readers Press®

Syracuse, New York
800.448.8878
www.newreaderspress.com